THE BEANIE ENCYCLOPEDIA

A

T

688.7
Care

By [

COLLECTOR BOOKS
A Division of Schroeder Publishing Co., Inc.

The current values in this book should be used only as a guide. They are not intended to set prices, which vary from one section of the country to another. Auction prices as well as dealer prices vary greatly and are affected by condition as well as demand. Neither the Authors nor the Publisher assumes responsibility for any losses that might be incurred as a result of consulting this guide.

This book is not associated with or endorsed by Ty, Inc., McDonald's Corporation or any other distributors of Ty, Inc. dolls. Any rights in the trademark "Beanie Babies," the Ty heart logo, and any other Ty logos, names or marks depicted in photographs of Ty, Inc. dolls and/or the trademarks "Happy Meal," "Teenie Beanies," and any other logos, names or marks used by McDonald's Corporation or other distributors of Ty, Inc. dolls are owned by Ty, Inc., McDonald's Corporation or other distributors of Ty, Inc. dolls. The authors and Schroeder Publishing Company, Inc. are not affiliated with Ty, Inc., McDonald's Corporation or any other distributors of Ty, Inc. dolls.

Searching for a Publisher?

We are always looking for knowledgeable people considered to be experts within their fields. If you feel that there is a real need for a book on your collectible subject and have a large comprehensive collection, contact Collector Books.

Please feel free to contact the author at the address below with new information, corrections, or questions for future editions.

On the cover:
Britannia — $600.00, Libearty — $400.00,
Glory — $100.00, Maple — $325.00

COLLECTOR BOOKS
P.O. Box 3009
Paducah, Kentucky 42002–3009

Carey Collectibles, Inc.
3623 Beach Drive
Tampa, Florida 33629
http://www.beanieencyclopedia.net

Copyright © 1998 by Carey Collectibles, Inc.

BEANIE BABIES*
A COLLECTING PHENOMENON

V

BEANIE BABIES* ARE HOT!!

**What started as a collectible for children has exploded
into a collecting phenomenon which has no bounds.**
Everyone is collecting. In the lines for Beanie Babies* you find kids
in strollers and grandparents with lists in hand.
**Everywhere you go you hear the Beanie Baby* buzz.
It's contagious!**

Last spring, a local store had people camp out the night before
for a chance to buy Peace the Bear. In the morning,
when the store opened, 170 people were in line. It seems
no one can resist the hunt for these lovable Beanie Babies*.

Our exposure to Beanie Babies* came when we visited our niece,
Whitney Carey, in McHenry, Illinois. She showed us her collection
and we were hooked. First, our goal was to collect one of each of
the current Beanie Babies*. Soon, all five of our children wanted
their own collection. Later, we expanded into retired Beanie
Babies*. Every night the phone would start ringing with our network of Beanie Baby* friends aiding us in our quest to collect every
Beanie Baby* for our **Beanie Encyclopedia**. Someone in the family
was always on the Internet looking, learning, or buying! It was a
family project which taught us the meaning of the term team work.

As a final note, we believe that one must remember that
Beanie Babies* are only toys. They were made for children
to play with, sleep with, dress in doll clothes, or just plain
carry around. Let your children play with the currents.
Our little cousins even take their Beanie Babies* in the bathtub!
Put aside the Beanie Babies* you want to collect but don't
forget to give the children the chance to love them as toys.

Enjoy your collection. But beware, it's contagious! As our
family says, "It's an illness and the whole family caught it!"

Dr. Beanie™
Susan S. Carey, DMD
July 1998

CONTENTS

· ·

ABOUT THE AUTHORS

Dr. Beanie™, Dr. Susan Carey, and her children Ryan, 17; Tara, 12; Kelly, 10; Megan, 7; and Kyle, 4; have been avid Beanie Baby* collectors for several years. What started as a small family hobby mushroomed into a crazy, fun-filled endeavor to share their knowledge and passion with others. The Careys reside in Tampa, Florida, with Dad, Michael, and a house full of birds, tropical fish, and of course Beanie Babies™!

THE ORIGINAL 9
BEANIE BABIES*

In 1994, Ty Inc.* introduced the original nine Beanie Babies*. They were Legs the Frog, Patti the Platypus, Splash the Whale, Flash the Dolphin, Spot the Dog, Chocolate the Moose, Cubbie the Bear, Squealer the Pig, and Pinchers the Lobster.

1

THE BEANIE BABY* STORY
WITH A DREAM, BEANIE BABIES* WERE BORN

The genius behind the Beanie Babies* sensation is H. Ty Warner, founder of Ty Inc.* Mr. Warner is a graduate of Kalamazoo College in Kalamazoo, Michigan. For many years he worked for Dakin, Inc., so he was very experienced with the stuffed animal business. In 1986, he founded Ty Inc.* in Oakbrook, Illinois. Ty Inc.'s* first product lines were the Himalayan Cats and collectible teddy bears.

Ty had a vision of a collectible toy product for children which was small enough to be held in their hands and priced so they could purchase it with their allowance money. With that dream, Beanie Babies* were born. Beanie Babies* production began in 1993 and they were officially issued January 8, 1994. The original nine Beanie Babies* were Chocolate the Moose, Cubbie the Brown Bear, Flash the Dolphin, Legs the Frog, Patti the Platypus (raspberry), Pinchers the Lobster, Splash the Whale, Spot the Dog (without a spot), and Squealer the Pig.

· ·

Ty Inc.'s* unique marketing approach was to limit vendors selling its product to small gift or toy stores, floral shops, and Hallmark* stores. They avoided using bigger stores such as Toys "Я" Us, Kmart, or Wal-Mart.

· ·

After a slow start, sales increased, especially in the Chicago area. As the demand increased, the Beanie Babies* became harder to find. The Beanie Baby* craze was here. To fuel the fire, Ty Inc.* began retiring and issuing new Beanie Babies*. As new Beanie Babies* were released, people couldn't wait to buy them. By 1997, the mania was in full force. Product disappeared instantly from store shelves. Ty Inc.'s* erratic shipping of product was ingenious. Vendors and customers waited anxiously for that UPS truck. With their scarcity, the Beanie Baby* secondary market was born.

People turned to the Internet for Beanie Baby* information. Much credit goes to Beanie Mom, Sara Nelson, for her devotion in estab-

lishing a quality, fact-filled website for Beanie Baby* collectors to gain information. In August 1996, Ty Inc.* also entered cyberspace with their own web page. Now, collectors had a direct source to Ty Inc's* information.

Collectors also turned to the Internet to sell and purchase Beanie Babies*. In this book, we have a comprehensive listing of current Internet sites for the Beanie Baby* enthusiast.

· ·

Check out our web page at:
http://www.beanieencyclopedia.net

· ·

Even McDonald's got involved in the excitement and Beanie Baby* craze. When they began their Teenie Beanies* Happy Meal* promotion in April 1997, the whole world learned about Beanie Babies* overnight. Adults gravitated toward these adorable collectibles. Many McDonald's* sold out of their entire week's supply of Teenie Beanies* the first day of the promotion. There were traffic jams on roads by McDonald's* restaurants and in some instances police were needed to control traffic problems. Many McDonald's* set Happy Meal* purchase limits and limited the purchase of extra Teenie Beanies*. The long lines and commotion were covered by the news media. With all of the publicity, the demand for all Beanie Babies* skyrocketed.

· · · · · · · · · · 2 · · · · · · · · · ·

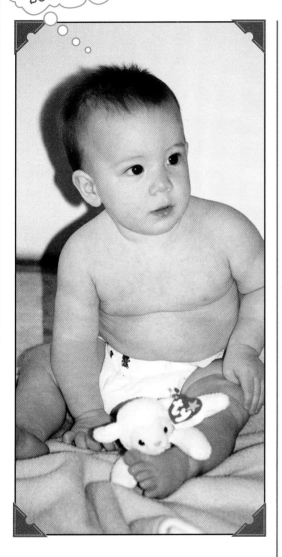

"It feels good to collect Beanie Babies."*

No one truly knows the future of Beanie Baby* collecting. We are often asked **"Is it a fad?"** We believe that the future of Beanie Baby* collecting will be strong for several reasons...

1. Both adults and children are collecting. Beanie Babies* appeal to all age groups.

2. The secondary market is extremely strong. Prices continue to escalate.

3. Ty Inc.* recently hired two top executives from Enesco. Both men have strong experience in the promotion of collectibles.

4. Obviously, Beanie Babies* have been unbelievably profitable for Ty Inc.* We can expect them to continue with new releases and retirements.

5. Children love to play with Beanie Babies*. History shows that children grow up to collect that which they played with as a child. (Yes, we have a Barbie doll collection in this house.)

6. Ty Inc.* has established a collectors' club. The **Beanie Babies* Official Club** began spring 1998. Other collectibles with collectors' clubs have had a solid history of longevity.

7. Beanie Babies* are priced where anyone can afford to purchase one.

8. Beanie Babies* are truly irresistible. Once you start collecting, it is contagious!

Most importantly, collecting Beanie Babies* is fun.
Ty Inc.* has produced a toy that brings a smile to faces young and old.
It feels good to collect Beanie Babies*.
Yes, indeed, the future of Beanie Babies* appears great.
Ty Warner's dream will continue to bring joy for years to come.

BEANIE BABIES*
BUYING · SELLING · COLLECTING

BUYING • SELLING • COLLECTING
THE DEMAND IS GREATER THAN THE SUPPLY

- Beanie Babies* can be purchased at over 60,000 Ty* vendors.

- Most vendors sell the Beanie Babies* for $5.00 – $7.00.

- Beanie Babies* can be found at small toy and gift shops, florists, hospital gift shops, airport stores, and other collectible shops.

Specifically, they are found in Hallmarks*, Noodle Kidoodles*, Cracker Barrels*, and Nordstroms*. Ty Inc.* has been reducing the number of vendors. The vendors also receive very erratic shipments of product. Ty Inc.* greatly controls the ordering by these vendors both by limiting Beanie Baby* types and quantities. Almost always the demand is greater than the supply. This is especially true of new releases.

This demand triggered the growth of the secondary market. A secondary market is the sale of Beanie Babies* through unofficial dealers. They are found in stores, at flea markets, collectible shows and conventions, or through the mail-order companies or newspaper advertisements. Perhaps the most action takes place on the Internet where dealing goes on around the clock. We recommend you utilize the trusted Beanie Baby* Internet sites listed in the **Internet Section** of this book and beware as fraud has occurred with some Internet transactions.

> **We recommend you utilize the trusted Beanie Baby* Internet sites listed in the Internet Section of this book as fraud has occurred with some Internet transactions.**

"Around-the-clock action on the Internet"

Buying • Selling • Collecting
Values - Being Aware of Conditions

To buy or sell Beanie Babies* one must be aware of the classifications of Beanie Baby* condition. Most values given in price guides, including this book, are for mint Beanie Babies* with both hang tag and tush tag in perfect condition. When selling to a dealer don't expect to get full price. Dealers must realize a profit. Most dealers purchase Beanie Babies* at 60 – 80% of value.

With Hang Tag
<u>Mint</u> — 100% – 120% of value
A mint Beanie Baby* is in perfect condition. The hang tag has no bends, no creases, no sign of wear, no writing on the tags or Beanie Baby*, and no tearing around the fastener hole. In other words, the Beanie Baby* looks like the day it was first put on the store shelf.
<u>Near Mint</u> — 50 – 80% of mint value
The hang tag may have slight wear around fastener hole and/or a slight crease that doesn't show white.
Without Hang Tags
Beanie Babies* without hang tags (but with tush tags) are valued 25 – 50% of the mint value.
Tush Tags
Beanie Babies* without tush tags are valued 10 – 25% of the mint value.
Writing on the tush tag decreases the value of the Beanie Baby* by 75%.

The price of a Beanie Baby* is totally dependent on the basic law of economics, the law of supply and demand. With high demand, the Beanie Baby* becomes more scarce which drives the price up. New releases are always scarce initially, which causes higher initial prices. For instance, Gobbles the Turkey was selling for $50 – $75 when first released; but as the supply increased, his price went down. Eventually, Gobbles could be found for under $10.

Status
The status of the Beanie Baby* also affects price.
Current:
Currently produced and shipped by Ty Inc.*
Retired:
Ty Inc.* has announced the Beanie Baby* will no longer be produced and the Beanie Baby* will never be produced again in the future. Prior to 1997, Ty Inc.* did not announce retirements of Beanie Babies*, they just stopped shipping them.
Out of Production:
Often a Beanie Baby* is no longer produced by Ty Inc.* Most discontinued Beanie Babies* are considered retired.

Style Changes
Many Beanie Babies* have changed appearance over time. When a style change occurs, the older style is out of production and is considered retired. For example, in 1998 Derby came out with a star on his forehead. The original coarse mane Derby is now considered retired. Other Beanie Babies* that have had style changes are Patti, Zip, Nip, Happy, Peanut, Quackers, Digger, Tank, Lucky, Lizzy, Magic, Inky, Spot, Mystic, Sly, Stripes, Bongo, Inch, and the Teddies.

· · · · · · · · · · · 6 · · · · · · · · · · · ·

Beanie Babies* should be kept out of direct sunlight in an enclosed container to limit dust. Do not store in air-tight baggies or plastic cases as mold and mildew will grow on Beanie Babies*. Also avoid damp garages or attics for storage. For best resale value they should be in a smoke-free environment.

Display your Beanie Babies* so you and others can enjoy them. The most popular method is in an enclosed glass-door curio cabinet. Other creative displays are Beanie Baby* shelves, houses, ladders, acrylic cubes, and even giant Noah's arks. Of course two of each Beanie Baby* is a must for the ark!

If soiled, most Beanie Babies* can be cleaned. It is safe to wash most Beanie Babies* by hand or in the washing machine. Always remove the paper hang tag first.

. . . .

To hand wash a Beanie Baby*, use a mild detergent in warm water. Rinse and dry. If using a washing machine, place the Beanie Baby* in a pillowcase and tie it shut. Use the most gentle cycle. Beanie Babies* can be dried in a dryer in the pillowcase on a low-heat cycle. Air drying or a hand-held hair blow dryer will work. After drying, fluff the fabric with a toothbrush.

. . . .

Some Beanie Babies* cannot be washed. These include any Beanie Babies* with felt pieces. Do not submerse Seaweed, Doodle, Strut, Lizzy, Slither, Lucky, Grunt, Tank, Crunch, Radar, Wise, Batty, Bucky, and Spooky with felt mouth. Difficult stains and Beanie Babies* of value should be cleaned only by a professional.

Tag protectors are a must. Numerous styles of tag protectors are available. Some collectors prefer to remove their tags for safe keeping. These tags can be reattached at a later date when the Beanie Baby* is sold or

"Tag protectors are a must! Keep me clean!"

traded. This has become an acceptable practice with collectors. However, buyer beware, make sure any Beanie Baby* you purchase has the correct tag attached.

Price stickers on Beanie Babies* are part of the history of the Beanie Baby* and should not reduce the value. Many collectors do avoid collecting Beanie Babies* with price stickers or prefer to remove them. Since removing the sticker may damage the hang tag, we recommend leaving stickers on the tag. When selling or trading a Beanie Baby* with a price sticker, the buyer should be told.

To remove a price sticker, first soften the glue by blowing warm air on it from a hair dryer on the low setting. Continue until the sticker can be easily removed with care. If any glue remains, use a solvent (such as lighter fluid) to remove the film of glue. Beware, as the ink from the hang tag can easily be ruined.

THE COMPLETE
BEANIE BABY*
COLLECTION

 **BEANIE** R_x

The material on Ally's back is the same material as Speedy's shell and Slither's back. In March 1998, Ally's value rose considerably. People started buying up many of the October retirees which led to the dramatic price change. Try to locate Ally with a 1st or 2nd generation hang tag as they are appreciating rapidly in value.

ALLY  *

The Alligator ▪ #4032

ESTIMATED PRODUCTION: 1,750,000

STATUS: Retired, 10-1-97

INTRODUCED: 1994 ▪ BIRTHDAY: 3-14-94

HANG TAG	VALUE 7/1/97	VALUE 1/1/98	VALUE 7/1/98
1ST Generation	$75	$200	$475
2ND Generation	$45	$100	$300
3RD Generation	$30	$75	$130
4TH Generation	$10	$30	$65
5TH Generation	–	–	–

ANTS *

The Anteater ▪ #4195

ESTIMATED RETIREMENT: 2001
STATUS: Current
INTRODUCED: 5-30-98 ▪ BIRTHDAY: 11-7-97

Rx

Ants the Anteater is so ugly that he is cute. Immediately popular with young boys, we expect his popularity to grow. Ants was given a premature announcement on a few web sites such as BeanieMom.com and ToysforToddlers.com about two weeks before the official announcement.

HANG TAG	VALUE 7/1/97	VALUE 1/1/98	VALUE 7/1/98
1ST Generation	–	–	–
2ND Generation	–	–	–
3RD Generation	–	–	–
4TH Generation	–	–	–
5TH Generation	–	–	$15

The tan tail Bongo is a current Beanie Baby*, however, not many 3rd generation tan tailed Bongos were produced. The Bongo with a black and white tush tag commands the highest dollar amount of all the Bongos. Look for Bongo to be retired next year. Bongo was initially produced as Nana.

Rx

BONGO*

The Monkey with the Tan Tail ▪ #4067

ESTIMATED RETIREMENT: 1999

STATUS: Current

INTRODUCED: 1995 ▪ BIRTHDAY: 8-17-95

HANG TAG	VALUE 7/1/97	VALUE 1/1/98	VALUE 7/1/98
1ST Generation	–	–	–
2ND Generation	–	–	–
3RD Generation	$50	$100	$175
4TH Generation	$10	$10	$10
5TH Generation	–	–	$10

BRITANNIA*

The Bear ▪ #4601

ESTIMATED RETIREMENT: 1999

STATUS: Current

INTRODUCED: 1-1-98 ▪ BIRTHDAY: 12-15-97

HANG TAG	VALUE 7/1/97	VALUE 1/1/98	VALUE 7/1/98
1ST Generation	–	–	–
2ND Generation	–	–	–
3RD Generation	–	–	–
4TH Generation	–	–	–
5TH Generation	–	–	$600

Rx

A European exclusive, Britannia is highly sought after due to a smaller number of Britannias produced. People in the U.S. have paid as high as $1,000 to get their hands on Britannia. She will never be available anywhere but Europe.

Rx

Bronty is made out of a bluish tie-dyed material that can also be found on Sting, Rainbow, and Hissy. When produced, his fabric kept splitting at the seams. Because of this, he is harder to find and more sought after than his other dinosaur counterparts.

BRONTY*

The Brontosaurus ▪ #4085

ESTIMATED PRODUCTION: 50,000

STATUS: Retired, 6-15-96

INTRODUCED: 1995 ▪ BIRTHDAY: Unknown

HANG TAG	VALUE 7/1/97	VALUE 1/1/98	VALUE 7/1/98
1ST Generation	–	–	–
2ND Generation	–	–	–
3RD Generation	$400	$600	$1,300
4TH Generation	–	–	–
5TH Generation	–	–	–

BROWNIE*

The Brown Bear ▪ #4010
ESTIMATED PRODUCTION: 1,000
STATUS: Retired, 1993
INTRODUCED: 1993 ▪ BIRTHDAY: Unknown

The Beanie Babies Collection
Brownie ™ Style 4010
©1993 Ty Inc. Oakbrook, IL. USA
All Rights Reserved. Caution:
Remove this tag before giving
toy to a child. For ages 5 and up.
Handmade in Korea.
Surface
Wash.

HANG TAG	VALUE 7/1/97	VALUE 1/1/98	VALUE 7/1/98
1ST Generation	$1,000	$2,000	$5,200
2ND Generation	–	–	–
3RD Generation	–	–	–
4TH Generation	–	–	–
5TH Generation	–	–	–

Rx

Brownie is the first version of Cubbie. He was made before the original nine were introduced in 1994. Because of this, many collectors consider him a prototype. We consider him part of the retired Beanie Baby* family. He is an excellent Beanie Baby* to buy if you can afford his price. Brownie was only produced in Korea with a first generation hang tag. Without the hang tag that reads "Brownie* style 4010" he is worth less than $10. Nothing else distinguishes him from a tagless Cubbie.

 **DR. BEANIE**

Rx

Bruno and Spunky were the fifteenth and sixteenth dogs introduced into the Beanie Baby* family. Their arrival was announced on January 1, 1998.

Bruno has not been a popular Beanie Baby*. He is often one of the last Beanie Babies* left on the shelves.

BRUNO*

The Terrier ▪ #4183

ESTIMATED RETIREMENT: 2003

STATUS: Current

INTRODUCED: 1-1-98 ▪ BIRTHDAY: 9-9-97

HANG TAG	VALUE 7/1/97	VALUE 1/1/98	VALUE 7/1/98
1ST Generation	–	–	–
2ND Generation	–	–	–
3RD Generation	–	–	–
4TH Generation	–	–	–
5TH Generation	–	–	$10

BUBBLES*

The Black and Yellow Fish ▪ #4078

ESTIMATED PRODUCTION: 750,000

STATUS: Retired, 5-11-97

INTRODUCED: 1995 ▪ BIRTHDAY: 7-2-95

HANG TAG	VALUE 7/1/97	VALUE 1/1/98	VALUE 7/1/98
1ST Generation	–	–	–
2ND Generation	–	–	–
3RD Generation	$75	$135	$260
4TH Generation	$35	$85	$185
5TH Generation	–	–	–

R

Bubbles is one of the three fish in the Beanie Baby* family. Her material is leftover from Bumble the Bee. Since all three fish are retired, look for a new fish to be produced in the near future.

*Trademark or name of Ty, Inc., McDonald's Corporation or other distributors of Ty, Inc. dolls, not affiliated with the authors or Schroeder Publishing.

BEANIE
DR.

Rx

Bucky was retired on January 1, 1998. Although Bucky was never considered hard to find, once he retired he seemed to disappear. Everyone started scrambling for him. Bucky is a good buy at today's prices. We expect his value to greatly increase over time.

BUCKY*

The Beaver ▪ #4016

ESTIMATED PRODUCTION: 3,000,000
STATUS: Retired, 1-1-98
INTRODUCED: 1996 ▪ BIRTHDAY: 6-8-95

HANG TAG	VALUE 7/1/97	VALUE 1/1/98	VALUE 7/1/98
1ST Generation	–	–	–
2ND Generation	–	–	–
3RD Generation	$30	$60	$110
4TH Generation	$10	$20	$40
5TH Generation	–	–	$40

BUMBLE*

The Bee ▪ #4045

ESTIMATED PRODUCTION: 100,000
STATUS: Retired, 6-15-96
INTRODUCED: 1995 ▪ BIRTHDAY: 10-16-95

HANG TAG	VALUE 7/1/97	VALUE 1/1/98	VALUE 7/1/98
1ST Generation	–	–	–
2ND Generation	–	–	–
3RD Generation	$175	$400	$700
4TH Generation	$200	$450	$800
5TH Generation	–	–	–

Rx

Bumble was retired very shortly after he was released with a 4th generation hang tag. Because of this, Bumble with a 4th generation hang tag is more sought after and more valuable than Bumble with a 3rd generation hang tag. Bumble is made of the same material as Bubbles. According to Ty Inc.*, this bee was officially retired on June 15, 1996, along with Caw, Bronty, Flutter, Rex, and Steg.

*Trademark or name of Ty, Inc., McDonald's Corporation or other distributors of Ty, Inc. dolls, not affiliated with the authors or Schroeder Publishing.

R_x

Caw's body style is almost identical to Kiwi's. According to Ty Inc.*, both Caw and Bumble retired on June 15, 1996. That leads us to wonder why Caws cannot be found with a 4th generation hang tag yet Bumbles have them.

CAW *

The Crow ▪ #4071

ESTIMATED PRODUCTION: 100,000
STATUS: Retired, 6-15-96
INTRODUCED: 1995 ▪ BIRTHDAY: Unknown

HANG TAG	VALUE 7/1/97	VALUE 1/1/98	VALUE 7/1/98
1ST Generation	–	–	–
2ND Generation	–	–	–
3RD Generation	$200	$400	$900
4TH Generation	–	–	–
5TH Generation	–	–	–

CHILLY*

The Polar Bear • #4012

ESTIMATED PRODUCTION: 25,000

STATUS: Retired, 1-7-96

INTRODUCED: 1994 • BIRTHDAY: Unknown

HANG TAG	VALUE 7/1/97	VALUE 1/1/98	VALUE 7/1/98
1ST Generation	$750	$1,400	$2,600
2ND Generation	$725	$1,350	$2,550
3RD Generation	$700	$1,300	$2,500
4TH Generation	–	–	–
5TH Generation	–	–	–

Chilly is one of the five lying down bears in the Beanie Baby* family. He is difficult to find in mint condition because his white coat is very hard to keep clean. If possible keep Chilly in an enclosed container to avoid dust. As time goes by, there will be fewer mint Chillys to be found.

 **Rx**

Chip was difficult to find in 1997 but more showed up on the store shelves in early 1998. Chip is still not an easy find so don't feel badly if you have to pay a few dollars more for her at a secondary store.

The Calico Cat ▪ #4121

ESTIMATED RETIREMENT: 1999
STATUS: Current
INTRODUCED: 5-11-97 ▪ BIRTHDAY: 1-26-96

HANG TAG	VALUE 7/1/97	VALUE 1/1/98	VALUE 7/1/98
1ST Generation	–	–	–
2ND Generation	–	–	–
3RD Generation	–	–	–
4TH Generation	$10	$10	$10
5TH Generation	–	–	$10

CHOCOLATE *

The Moose ▪ #4015

ESTIMATED RETIREMENT: 1999
STATUS: Current
INTRODUCED: 1994 ▪ BIRTHDAY: 4-27-93

HANG TAG	VALUE 7/1/97	VALUE 1/1/98	VALUE 7/1/98
1ST Generation	$75	$175	$350
2ND Generation	$45	$75	$200
3RD Generation	$30	$45	$100
4TH Generation	$10	$10	$10
5TH Generation	–	–	$10

R

One variation of Chocolate's poem tag has a second line that has moose spelled "rnoose." Chocolate was one of the original nine Beanie Babies* and is highly sought after with a first generation hang tag. He is the only original nine member to not be retired. Expect him to retire soon.

 **BEANIE**

Rx

Since his introduction, Bernie has been a favorite of collectors. Dogs must be a favorite of Ty Inc.* too, with 19 dogs in the Beanie baby* family. Will there be more dogs to come?

BERNIE*

The St. Bernard ▪ #4109

ESTIMATED RETIREMENT: 2002

STATUS: Current

INTRODUCED: 1-1-97 ▪ BIRTHDAY: 10-3-96

HANG TAG	VALUE 7/1/97	VALUE 1/1/98	VALUE 7/1/98
1ST Generation	–	–	–
2ND Generation	–	–	–
3RD Generation	–	–	–
4TH Generation	$10	$10	$10
5TH Generation	–	–	$10

BESSIE *

The Brown and White Cow ▪ #4009

ESTIMATED PRODUCTION: 1,500,000
STATUS: Retired, 10-1-97
INTRODUCED: 1995 ▪ BIRTHDAY: 6-27-95

HANG TAG	VALUE 7/1/97	VALUE 1/1/98	VALUE 7/1/98
1ST Generation	–	–	–
2ND Generation	–	–	–
3RD Generation	$30	$75	$130
4TH Generation	$8	$40	$70
5TH Generation	–	–	–

*Trademark or name of Ty, Inc., McDonald's Corporation or other distributors of Ty, Inc. dolls, not affiliated with the authors or Schroeder Publishing.

Bessie is one of two cows in the Beanie Babies* family (along with Daisy). Bessie is the fourth most valuable October 1997 retiree, after Seamore, Teddy, and Tank. Expect Bessie's value to rise as the January and May 1997 retirees go up in value and become too expensive for many collectors.

 **BEANIE**

R_x

Blackie is one of the five lying down bears in the Beanie Baby* family, along with Brownie, Chilly, Cubbie, and Peking. Don't expect Blackie to be around much longer.

BLACKIE*

The Black Bear ▪ #4011

ESTIMATED RETIREMENT: 1999

STATUS: Current

INTRODUCED: 1994 ▪ BIRTHDAY: 7-15-94

HANG TAG	VALUE 7/1/97	VALUE 1/1/98	VALUE 7/1/98
1ST Generation	$75	$150	$325
2ND Generation	$45	$75	$225
3RD Generation	$30	$45	$90
4TH Generation	$10	$10	$10
5TH Generation	–	–	$10

BLIZZARD*

The Black and White Tiger ▪ #4163

ESTIMATED PRODUCTION: 2,500,000

STATUS: Retired, 5-1-98

INTRODUCED: 5-11-97 ▪ BIRTHDAY: 12-12-96

HANG TAG	VALUE 7/1/97	VALUE 1/1/98	VALUE 7/1/98
1ST Generation	–	–	–
2ND Generation	–	–	–
3RD Generation	–	–	–
4TH Generation	$20	$10	$25
5TH Generation	–	–	$25

DR. BEANIE

R

For months, it was rumored that Blizzard would have a name change to Snowflake. Rumors started that a trademark problem with Dairy Queen was causing the name change. This rumor has been proven wrong. Blizzard, now retired, was often a difficult Beanie Baby* to locate. Expect her to increase in value quickly.

*Trademark or name of Ty, Inc., McDonald's Corporation or other distributors of Ty, Inc. dolls, not affiliated with the authors or Schroeder Publishing.

BONES*

The Brown Dog ■ #4001

ESTIMATED PRODUCTION: 3,500,000
STATUS: Retired, 5-1-98
INTRODUCED: 1994 ■ BIRTHDAY: 1-18-94

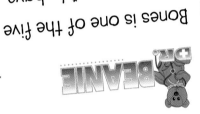

Bones is one of the five Beanie Babies* to have come with all five genera-tion hang tags. Spot with-out a spot is the only dog older than Bones.

HANG TAG	VALUE 7/1/97	VALUE 1/1/98	VALUE 7/1/98
1st Generation	$75	$150	$395
2nd Generation	$45	$75	$285
3rd Generation	$30	$45	$145
4th Generation	$10	$10	$25
5th Generation	–	–	$25

BONGO*

The Monkey with the Brown Tail ▪ #4067

ESTIMATED PRODUCTION: 500,000

STATUS: Retired, 6-29-96

INTRODUCED: 1996 ▪ BIRTHDAY: 8-17-95

R̸

Bongo's tail color has changed several times between brown and tan. The brown tail version should appreciate greatly if it is officially retired. It currently is out of production but it is impossible to know if the brown tail will be reinstated.

HANG TAG	VALUE 7/1/97	VALUE 1/1/98	VALUE 7/1/98
1ST Generation	–	–	–
2ND Generation	–	–	–
3RD Generation	$100	$75	$150
4TH Generation	$10	$35	$75
5TH Generation	–	–	–

 **BEANIE**

℞

At a January 1998 Philadelphia 76ers basketball game, Baldy was given out to children. See the Special Promotions Section of this book on page 227 for more details.

BALDY *

The Eagle ▪ #4074

ESTIMATED PRODUCTION: 3,500,000
STATUS: Retired, 5-1-98
INTRODUCED: 5-11-97 ▪ BIRTHDAY: 2-17-96

HANG TAG	VALUE 7/1/97	VALUE 1/1/98	VALUE 7/1/98
1ST Generation	–	–	–
2ND Generation	–	–	–
3RD Generation	–	–	–
4TH Generation	$10	$10	$25
5TH Generation	–	–	$25

*Trademark or name of Ty, Inc., McDonald's Corporation or other distributors of Ty, Inc. dolls, not affiliated with the authors or Schroeder Publishing.

BATTY*

The Bat ▪ #4035

ESTIMATED RETIREMENT: 2000
STATUS: Current
INTRODUCED: 10-1-97 ▪ BIRTHDAY: 10-29-96

HANG TAG	VALUE 7/1/97	VALUE 1/1/98	VALUE 7/1/98
1ST Generation	–	–	–
2ND Generation	–	–	–
3RD Generation	–	–	–
4TH Generation	–	$25	$10
5TH Generation	–	–	$10

Batty was introduced on October 1, 1997, as one of the five holiday Beanie Babies*. He is the second bat in the Beanie Baby* collection and is a good replacement for the retired Radar. Batty is the first Beanie Baby* to use Velcro. On May 31, 1998, Batty was presented to children at a Milwaukee Brewers game. See page 233 for details.

 **R**

Chops was retired in January 1997 and was replaced by Fleece. There were many fake Chops circulating in late 1997. These counterfeit Chops were poorly reproduced and have several discrepancies. The tags were also not well made (make sure you inspect all Beanie Babies* before buying them and only buy from reputable dealers). See the Counterfeit Section on page 268 of this book for details.

CHOPS*

The Lamb ▪ #4019

ESTIMATED PRODUCTION: 500,000

STATUS: Retired, 1-1-97

INTRODUCED: 1996 ▪ BIRTHDAY: 5-3-96

HANG TAG	VALUE 7/1/97	VALUE 1/1/98	VALUE 7/1/98
1ST Generation	–	–	–
2ND Generation	–	–	–
3RD Generation	$90	$120	$260
4TH Generation	$55	$95	$190
5TH Generation	–	–	–

*Trademark or name of Ty, Inc., McDonald's Corporation or other distributors of Ty, Inc. dolls, not affiliated with the authors or Schroeder Publishing.

CLAUDE*

The Tie-Dyed Crab ▪ #4083

ESTIMATED RETIREMENT: 1999
STATUS: Current
INTRODUCED: 5-11-97 ▪ BIRTHDAY: 9-3-96

HANG TAG	VALUE 7/1/97	VALUE 1/1/98	VALUE 7/1/98
1ST Generation	–	–	–
2ND Generation	–	–	–
3RD Generation	–	–	–
4TH Generation	$10	$10	$10
5TH Generation	–	–	$10

Rx

Watch for Claude's life to be short lived. Tie-dyed Beanie Babies* tend to be great retirement candidates. Claude became the third crab in the Beanie Baby* family, after the orange and red Diggers. Claude's fabric is unique to the Beanie Baby* family.

 **Dr. BEANIE**

Rx

Congo was originally extremely hard to find. Summer 1997, he was selling for $35 on the secondary market. Now he is priced as an average current Beanie Baby* due to his availability in stores. Congo was featured as a promotion at the 1998 New York Toy Fair. See the Special Promotions Section on page 236 of this book for details.

CONGO*

The Gorilla ▪ #4160

ESTIMATED RETIREMENT: 2000
STATUS: Current
INTRODUCED: 1996 ▪ BIRTHDAY: 11-9-96

HANG TAG	VALUE 7/1/97	VALUE 1/1/98	VALUE 7/1/98
1ST Generation	–	–	–
2ND Generation	–	–	–
3RD Generation	–	–	–
4TH Generation	$35	$10	$10
5TH Generation	–	–	$10

CORAL*

The Tie-Dyed Fish ▪ #4079

ESTIMATED PRODUCTION: 350,000

STATUS: Retired, 1-1-97

INTRODUCED: 1996 ▪ BIRTHDAY: 3-2-95

HANG TAG	VALUE 7/1/97	VALUE 1/1/98	VALUE 7/1/98
1ST Generation	–	–	–
2ND Generation	–	–	–
3RD Generation	$85	$130	$300
4TH Generation	$55	$90	$220
5TH Generation	–	–	–

Coral was the last of the Beanie Baby* fish to be introduced (Goldie, mid-1994; Bubbles, mid-1995; and Coral, shortly after Bubbles). But, Coral was the first to retire (Coral, January 1997; Bubbles, May 1997; and Goldie, January 1998). Her beautiful tie-dyed colors of pinks, yellows, and blues make her a very popular Beanie Baby*. See page 267 for a picture of a counterfeit Coral.

*Trademark or name of Ty, Inc., McDonald's Corporation or other distributors of Ty, Inc. dolls, not affiliated with the authors or Schroeder Publishing.

One of the three worst sellers, along with Gracie and Snort, look for Crunch to be retired for this reason. He is a favorite of young boys but is seldom the Beanie Baby* of choice by young girls and adult collectors. Beware, washing this Beanie Baby* will damage his felt teeth. See page 7 in the Storage and Care section for more information.

CRUNCH*

The Shark ▪ #4130

ESTIMATED RETIREMENT: 1999

STATUS: Current

INTRODUCED: 1-1-97 ▪ BIRTHDAY: 1-13-96

HANG TAG	VALUE 7/1/97	VALUE 1/1/98	VALUE 7/1/98
1ST Generation	–	–	–
2ND Generation	–	–	–
3RD Generation	–	–	–
4TH Generation	$10	$10	$10
5TH Generation	–	–	$10

CUBBIE*

The Brown Bear ▪ #4010

ESTIMATED PRODUCTION: 3,000,000
STATUS: Retired, 1-1-98
INTRODUCED: 1994 ▪ BIRTHDAY: 11-14-93

HANG TAG	VALUE 7/1/97	VALUE 1/1/98	VALUE 7/1/98
1ST Generation	$75	$200	$550
2ND Generation	$45	$100	$250
3RD Generation	$30	$60	$110
4TH Generation	$10	$25	$35
5TH Generation	–	–	$35

Cubbie was one of the original nine Beanie Babies*. He replaced Brownie. The Beanie Baby* is exactly the same, only the tag was changed. Look for Cubbie with a rare 1st generation tag. Cubbie became even more popular because of the historical Chicago Cubs give-aways. See the Special Promotions Section on pages 225 – 227 of this book for details.

 **BEANIE**

R

Curly is definitely a retirement candidate. Get ahold of Curly now. He is one of the five napped Beanie Babies*. He is very difficult to find at retail stores. Once retired, expect his value to be quite high because of his lack of availability as a current, and his popularity with collectors. See page 243 for information on the Broadway Ragtime Curlys.

CURLY*

The Brown Napped Teddy ▪ #4052
ESTIMATED RETIREMENT: 1999
STATUS: Current
INTRODUCED: 1996 ▪ BIRTHDAY: 4-12-96

HANG TAG	VALUE 7/1/97	VALUE 1/1/98	VALUE 7/1/98
1ST Generation	–	–	–
2ND Generation	–	–	–
3RD Generation	–	–	–
4TH Generation	$25	$20	$18
5TH Generation	–	–	$18

*Trademark or name of Ty, Inc., McDonald's Corporation or other distributors of Ty, Inc. dolls, not affiliated with the authors or Schroeder Publishing.

DAISY*

The Black and White Cow ▪ #4006

ESTIMATED RETIREMENT: 2000
STATUS: Current
INTRODUCED: 1994 ▪ BIRTHDAY: 5-10-94

HANG TAG	VALUE 7/1/97	VALUE 1/1/98	VALUE 7/1/98
1ST Generation	$75	$150	$300
2ND Generation	$45	$75	$175
3RD Generation	$30	$45	$90
4TH Generation	$10	$10	$10
5TH Generation	–	–	$10

One of the two cows in the Beanie Baby* family, look for Daisy to be replaced by a new cow soon. Try to find Daisy with an original 1st generation hang tag. Daisy was distributed at the Chicago Cubs game on May 3, 1998, in honor of Harry Caray. See page 232 of the Special Promotion Section of this book.

*Trademark or name of Ty, Inc., McDonald's Corporation or other distributors of Ty, Inc. dolls, not affiliated with the authors or Schroeder Publishing.

 **BEANIE**
DR.

Rx

Fine-mane Derby was the original Derby. He was redesigned in 1996 to the coarse-mane Derby and had another style change in 1998 when the "star" was added to his forehead. He was supposedly changed because the fine pieces of yarn would easily unravel. If you think you have a fine-mane Derby, count the strands of yarn on his tail. Fine-mane has approximately 20 pieces. The coarse-mane has approximately 8.

DERBY*

The Fine-Mane Horse ▪ #4008

ESTIMATED PRODUCTION: 15,000
STATUS: Retired, 1995
INTRODUCED: 1995 ▪ BIRTHDAY: Unknown

HANG TAG	VALUE 7/1/97	VALUE 1/1/98	VALUE 7/1/98
1ST Generation	–	–	–
2ND Generation	–	–	–
3RD Generation	$400	$900	$4,800
4TH Generation	–	–	–
5TH Generation	–	–	–

DERBY*

The Coarse-Mane Horse ▪ #4008

ESTIMATED PRODUCTION: 2,500,000
STATUS: Retired, 12-15-97
INTRODUCED: 1995 ▪ BIRTHDAY: 9-16-95

HANG TAG	VALUE 7/1/97	VALUE 1/1/98	VALUE 7/1/98
1ST Generation	–	–	–
2ND Generation	–	–	–
3RD Generation	$65	$200	$1,500
4TH Generation	$10	$10	$25
5TH Generation	–	–	–

*Trademark or name of Ty, Inc., McDonald's Corporation or other distributors of Ty, Inc. dolls, not affiliated with the authors or Schroeder Publishing.

Rx

In January 1998, the coarse-mane Derby was replaced with a new Derby. The 3rd generation Derby tag is now highly sought after because it can be switched to a tagless fine-mane Derby. Most of the 3rd generation coarse-mane Derbys have manes that run much farther down their back than the 4th generation Derbys. This adds little value to the Beanie Baby* but is an interesting difference.

 **BEANIE**

℞

In January 1998, this new Derby with a "star" on his forehead replaced the coarse-mane Derby. This marked the second time Derby was changed. First he had a fine mane, next coarse mane, and finally coarse mane with the star. Derby with a star only comes with a 5th generation hang tag.

DERBY*

The Coarse-Mane Horse with Star ▪ #4008

ESTIMATED RETIREMENT: 2002

STATUS: Current

INTRODUCED: 12-31-97 ▪ BIRTHDAY: 9-16-95

HANG TAG	VALUE 7/1/97	VALUE 1/1/98	VALUE 7/1/98
1ST Generation	–	–	–
2ND Generation	–	–	–
3RD Generation	–	–	–
4TH Generation	–	–	–
5TH Generation	–	–	$10

DIGGER*

The Orange Crab ▪ #4027

ESTIMATED PRODUCTION: 50,000
STATUS: Retired, 6-3-95
INTRODUCED: 1994 ▪ BIRTHDAY: Unknown

DR. BEANIE

Rx

Digger was originally produced as an orange crab. She was later changed to the much more common red crab. Orange Digger, red Digger, and Claude share the exact same body style. Orange Digger was replaced by red Digger in mid-1995. She is a very good buy at the current market value. Her price should rise considerably once it is obvious how rare she is and how difficult she is to obtain.

HANG TAG	VALUE 7/1/97	VALUE 1/1/98	VALUE 7/1/98
1ST Generation	$350	$525	$1,000
2ND Generation	$325	$500	$950
3RD Generation	$300	$475	$900
4TH Generation	–	–	–
5TH Generation	–	–	–

*Trademark or name of Ty, Inc., McDonald's Corporation or other distributors of Ty, Inc. dolls, not affiliated with the authors or Schroeder Publishing.

RETIRED

Rx

Digger the red crab, replaced the orange Digger in mid-1995. She was retired in May of 1997 and was replaced by the tie-dyed Claude. Digger the red crab is the most common of the May 1997 retirees, but continues to sell well since the other May retirees have escalated in value and are priced out of reach to many collectors.

DIGGER[*]

The Red Crab ▪ #4027

ESTIMATED PRODUCTION: 1,000,000
STATUS: Retired, 5-11-97
INTRODUCED: 1995 ▪ BIRTHDAY: 8-23-95

HANG TAG	VALUE 7/1/97	VALUE 1/1/98	VALUE 7/1/98
1ST Generation	–	–	–
2ND Generation	–	–	–
3RD Generation	$50	$100	$400
4TH Generation	$25	$80	$125
5TH Generation	–	–	–

*Trademark or name of Ty, Inc., McDonald's Corporation or other distributors of Ty, Inc. dolls, not affiliated with the authors or Schroeder Publishing.

DOBY*

The Doberman ▪ #4110

ESTIMATED RETIREMENT: 2001
STATUS: Current

INTRODUCED: 1-1-97 ▪ BIRTHDAY: 10-6-96

HANG TAG	VALUE 7/1/97	VALUE 1/1/98	VALUE 7/1/98
1ST Generation	–	–	–
2ND Generation	–	–	–
3RD Generation	–	–	–
4TH Generation	$10	$10	$10
5TH Generation	–	–	$10

R

Doby was the first name released to be one of the May 1998 McDonald's* Teenie Beanies*. Doby was number one of the twelve Beanie Baby* set. Doby, one of the 19 Beanie Baby* family dogs, has not been as popular with collectors as first expected.

*Trademark or name of Ty, Inc., McDonald's Corporation or other distributors of Ty, Inc. dolls, not affiliated with the authors or Schroeder Publishing.

Rx

Doodle's name was rumored to have been changed to Strut because of a trademark conflict with Chick-Fil-A. The name Doodle was retired even though the Beanie Baby* itself was not retired. Doodle and Strut are identical Beanie Babies* except for the tags.

DOODLE*

The Rooster ▪ #4171

ESTIMATED PRODUCTION: 1,500,000

STATUS: Retired, 8-97

INTRODUCED: 5-11-97 ▪ BIRTHDAY: 3-8-96

HANG TAG	VALUE 7/1/97	VALUE 1/1/98	VALUE 7/1/98
1ST Generation	–	–	–
2ND Generation	–	–	–
3RD Generation	–	–	–
4TH Generation	$10	$40	$60
5TH Generation	–	–	–

*Trademark or name of Ty, Inc., McDonald's Corporation or other distributors of Ty, Inc. dolls, not affiliated with the authors or Schroeder Publishing.

DOTTY*

The Dalmatian with Black Ears ■ #4100

ESTIMATED RETIREMENT: 2001
STATUS: Current
INTRODUCED: 5-11-97 ■ BIRTHDAY: 10-17-96

HANG TAG	VALUE 7/1/97	VALUE 1/1/98	VALUE 7/1/98
1ST Generation	–	–	–
2ND Generation	–	–	–
3RD Generation	–	–	–
4TH Generation	$10	$10	$10
5TH Generation	–	–	$10

Dotty was a direct replacement for the retired Sparky. Rumor has it Sparky was retired because the name "Sparky" is a registered trademark of the National Fire Protection Association (N.F.P.A.). Dotty was a quick solution to the problem. The last Sparkys to hit the shelves actually had Dotty hang and tush tags. This acted as a premature announcement of the new Dalmatian. The only real difference is that Dotty has black ears and a black tail.

Ty Inc.* is always full of surprises. Collectors were surprised and thrilled when Ty Inc.* introduced six birds into the Beanie Baby* family on the same day. Early the Robin, Jake the Mallard Duck, Rocket the Blue Jay, Kuku the Cockatoo, Jabber the Parrot, and Wise the Owl were announced on Ty Inc's* website May 30, 1998.

EARLY *

The Robin ▪ #4190

ESTIMATED RETIREMENT: 2002
STATUS: Current
INTRODUCED: 5-30-98 ▪ BIRTHDAY: 3-20-97

HANG TAG	VALUE 7/1/97	VALUE 1/1/98	VALUE 7/1/98
1ST Generation	–	–	–
2ND Generation	–	–	–
3RD Generation	–	–	–
4TH Generation	–	–	–
5TH Generation	–	–	$15

EARS *

The Brown Rabbit ▪ #4018

ESTIMATED PRODUCTION: 3,500,000

STATUS: Retired, 5-1-98

INTRODUCED: 1996 ▪ BIRTHDAY: 4-18-95

    ℞

Ears was the only bunny in the Beanie Baby* family before the introduction of the Bunny trio – Hoppity, Hippity, and Floppity. Ears is the only lying down bunny. Collectors love his big lopped ears.

HANG TAG	VALUE 7/1/97	VALUE 1/1/98	VALUE 7/1/98
1ST Generation	–	–	–
2ND Generation	–	–	–
3RD Generation	$30	$45	$100
4TH Generation	$10	$10	$25
5TH Generation	–	–	$25

*Trademark or name of Ty, Inc., McDonald's Corporation or other distributors of Ty, Inc. dolls, not affiliated with the authors or Schroeder Publishing.

R_x

When first introduced, Echo and Waves had reversed tags. This mistake was corrected for the next shipment. The value of these Beanie Babies* should continue to appreciate.

ECHO*

The Dolphin ▪ #4180

ESTIMATED PRODUCTION: 3,500,000
STATUS: Retired, 5-1-98
INTRODUCED: 5-11-97 ▪ BIRTHDAY: 12-21-96

HANG TAG	VALUE 7/1/97	VALUE 1/1/98	VALUE 7/1/98
1ST Generation	–	–	–
2ND Generation	–	–	–
3RD Generation	–	–	–
4TH Generation	$10	$10	$25
5TH Generation	–	–	$25

*Trademark or name of Ty, Inc., McDonald's Corporation or other distributors of Ty, Inc. dolls, not affiliated with the authors or Schroeder Publishing.

ERIN *

The Bear ▪ #4186

ESTIMATED RETIREMENT: 1999
STATUS: Current
INTRODUCED: 1-31-98 ▪ BIRTHDAY: 3-17-97

HANG TAG	VALUE 7/1/97	VALUE 1/1/98	VALUE 7/1/98
1ST Generation	–	–	–
2ND Generation	–	–	–
3RD Generation	–	–	–
4TH Generation	–	–	–
5TH Generation	–	–	$70

Erin was introduced as yet another Beanie Baby* to commemorate a holiday. Rumors circulated that Erin would retire on St. Patrick's Day. Come March 17, Erin was still part of the current Beanie Baby* family. She was still difficult to find and was selling for $150. Hopefully, Ty Inc.* will continue to introduce more Teddies.

Rx

Since golden retrievers are one of the most popular dog breeds, Fetch has already proven to be in high demand. Many collectors only collect dogs.

See page 254 in the Collecting Groups section.

FETCH *

The Golden Retriever ▪ #4189

ESTIMATED RETIREMENT: 2002

STATUS: Current

INTRODUCED: 5-30-98 ▪ BIRTHDAY: 2-4-97

HANG TAG	VALUE 7/1/97	VALUE 1/1/98	VALUE 7/1/98
1ST Generation	–	–	–
2ND Generation	–	–	–
3RD Generation	–	–	–
4TH Generation	–	–	–
5TH Generation	–	–	$15

FLASH*

The Dolphin • #4021

ESTIMATED PRODUCTION: 1,000,000

STATUS: Retired, 5-11-97

INTRODUCED: 1994 • BIRTHDAY: 5-13-93

Flash was one of the original nine Beanie Babies*. Flash and her companion Splash were both retired in May 1997. They were replaced with the more sit up style Beanie Babies*, Echo and Waves, instead of the lying down style of Splash and Flash.

HANG TAG	VALUE 7/1/97	VALUE 1/1/98	VALUE 7/1/98
1ST Generation	$85	$225	$600
2ND Generation	$70	$150	$375
3RD Generation	$50	$100	$210
4TH Generation	$30	$80	$140
5TH Generation	–	–	–

*Trademark or name of Ty, Inc., McDonald's Corporation or other distributors of Ty, Inc. dolls, not affiliated with the authors or Schroeder Publishing.

Rx

Fleece was a replacement for the retired Chops. She joins Curly, Scottie, Gigi, and Tuffy as the only napped Beanie Babies*.

FLEECE*

The Napped Lamb ▪ #4125

ESTIMATED RETIREMENT: 1999

STATUS: Current

INTRODUCED: 1-1-97 ▪ BIRTHDAY: 3-21-96

HANG TAG	VALUE 7/1/97	VALUE 1/1/98	VALUE 7/1/98
1ST Generation	–	–	–
2ND Generation	–	–	–
3RD Generation	–	–	–
4TH Generation	$10	$10	$10
5TH Generation	–	–	$10

FLIP*

The White Cat ▪ #4012

ESTIMATED PRODUCTION: 2,000,000

STATUS: Retired, 10-1-97

INTRODUCED: 1996 ▪ BIRTHDAY: 2-28-95

Flip was retired on October 1, 1997. As soon as she retired, her value quickly jumped to about $25. This did not last long as many Ty Inc.* dealers received late shipments of Flip. This dropped her price. Flip's value finally started climbing again in March 1998. Look for another cat to join the retired family soon.

HANG TAG	VALUE 7/1/97	VALUE 1/1/98	VALUE 7/1/98
1ST Generation	–	–	–
2ND Generation	–	–	–
3RD Generation	$30	$75	$125
4TH Generation	$10	$25	$35
5TH Generation	–	–	–

*Trademark or name of Ty, Inc., McDonald's Corporation or other distributors of Ty, Inc. dolls, not affiliated with the authors or Schroeder Publishing.

Rx

Usually hard to find during most of the year, members of the Bunny trio, Floppity, Hoppity, and Hippity were more plentiful around Easter time. Now retired, expect the colored bunnies to appreciate in value. See the Special Interest Section on page 264 of this book for the Floppity prototype.

FLOPPITY*

The Lavender Bunny ▪ #4118

ESTIMATED PRODUCTION: 2,500,000

STATUS: Retired, 5-1-98

INTRODUCED: 1-1-97 ▪ BIRTHDAY: 5-28-96

HANG TAG	VALUE 7/1/97	VALUE 1/1/98	VALUE 7/1/98
1ST Generation	–	–	–
2ND Generation	–	–	–
3RD Generation	–	–	–
4TH Generation	$25	$10	$20
5TH Generation	–	–	$20

*Trademark or name of Ty, Inc., McDonald's Corporation or other distributors of Ty, Inc. dolls, not affiliated with the authors or Schroeder Publishing.

FLUTTER *

The Butterfly ▪ #4043

ESTIMATED PRODUCTION: 50,000
STATUS: Retired, 6-15-96
INTRODUCED: 1995 ▪ BIRTHDAY: Unknown

HANG TAG	VALUE 7/1/97	VALUE 1/1/98	VALUE 7/1/98
1ST Generation	–	–	–
2ND Generation	–	–	–
3RD Generation	$400	$650	$1,400
4TH Generation	–	–	–
5TH Generation	–	–	–

*Trademark or name of Ty, Inc., McDonald's Corporation or other distributors of Ty, Inc. dolls, not affiliated with the authors or Schroeder Publishing.

DR. BEANIE   Rx

Flutter was introduced in mid-1995. No two Flutters are identical. The colors found on Flutter are almost every color imaginable. Flutter is very rare and many collectors pay even more for one with bright beautiful coloring. Flutter was only made with a 3rd generation hang tag. He comes with both a 1995 black and white tush tag and a 1995 red and white no name tush tag.

 **DR. BEANIE**

℞

Collectors were thrilled with the introduction of Fortune the Panda. Peking, the retired panda, was a lying down version. Fortune is a sitting up bear which collectors seem to prefer. All sitting up bears have been good investments. Will you make a fortune with Fortune? No, but he is a prize for any collection.

FORTUNE *

The Panda Bear • #4196

ESTIMATED RETIREMENT: 2000
STATUS: Current
INTRODUCED: 5-30-98 ▪ BIRTHDAY: 10-6-97

HANG TAG	VALUE 7/1/97	VALUE 1/1/98	VALUE 7/1/98
1ST Generation	–	–	–
2ND Generation	–	–	–
3RD Generation	–	–	–
4TH Generation	–	–	–
5TH Generation	–	–	$75

57

FRECKLES *

The Leopard ▪ #4066

ESTIMATED RETIREMENT: 2000
STATUS: Current
INTRODUCED: 1996 ▪ BIRTHDAY: 6-3-96

HANG TAG	VALUE 7/1/97	VALUE 1/1/98	VALUE 7/1/98
1ST Generation	–	–	–
2ND Generation	–	–	–
3RD Generation	–	–	–
4TH Generation	$10	$10	$10
5TH Generation	–	–	$10

R̶x

Freckles was originally produced with a flat tail. Ty Inc.* since then has changed the tail to a more rounded version. Freckle's correct birthday is 6-3-96, however, some tags were made with a 7-28-96 birthday. This does not increase the value.

Rx

Garcia was rumored to have been retired due to a conflict with the estate of Jerry Garcia. Garcia's birthday is a combination of the month and day that Jerry Garcia was born and the year he died. When Garcia was retired he was replaced with the almost identical Peace.

GARCIA*

The Tie-Dyed Teddy • #4051

ESTIMATED PRODUCTION: 600,000
STATUS: Retired, 5-11-97
INTRODUCED: 1996 • BIRTHDAY: 8-1-95

HANG TAG	VALUE 7/1/97	VALUE 1/1/98	VALUE 7/1/98
1ST Generation	–	–	–
2ND Generation	–	–	–
3RD Generation	$105	$175	$250
4TH Generation	$65	$110	$200
5TH Generation	–	–	–

*Trademark or name of Ty, Inc., McDonald's Corporation or other distributors of Ty, Inc. dolls, not affiliated with the authors or Schroeder Publishing.

GIGI*

The Poodle ▪ #4191

ESTIMATED RETIREMENT: 2001
STATUS: Current
INTRODUCED: 5-30-98 ▪ BIRTHDAY: 4-7-97

HANG TAG	VALUE 7/1/97	VALUE 1/1/98	VALUE 7/1/98
1ST Generation	–	–	–
2ND Generation	–	–	–
3RD Generation	–	–	–
4TH Generation	–	–	–
5TH Generation	–	–	$15

Gigi the Poodle is the fifth napped Beanie Baby* along with Fleece, Scottie, Tuffy, and Curly. Gigi is very similar in appearance to Scottie. Gigi is the first Beanie Baby* to have two bows. She is also the first Beanie Baby* to contain both plush and napped material.

 **DR. BEANIE**

R_x

Of all of the May 30, 1998, introductions, Glory is the most sought after. Collectors hope she will follow in the footsteps of Libearty, which has greatly appreciated in value over time. Glory is the fourth Beanie Baby* to bear the American Flag along with Libearty, Lefty, and Righty.

GLORY*

The Bear ■ #4188

ESTIMATED RETIREMENT: 1999

STATUS: Current

INTRODUCED: 5-30-98 ■ BIRTHDAY: 7-4-97

HANG TAG	VALUE 7/1/97	VALUE 1/1/98	VALUE 7/1/98
1ST Generation	–	–	–
2ND Generation	–	–	–
3RD Generation	–	–	–
4TH Generation	–	–	–
5TH Generation	–	–	$100

*Trademark or name of Ty, Inc., McDonald's Corporation or other distributors of Ty, Inc. dolls, not affiliated with the authors or Schroeder Publishing.

61

GOBBLES*

The Turkey ▪ #4034

ESTIMATED RETIREMENT: 1999
STATUS: Current
INTRODUCED: 10-1-97 ▪ BIRTHDAY: 11-27-96

HANG TAG	VALUE 7/1/97	VALUE 1/1/98	VALUE 7/1/98
1ST Generation	–	–	–
2ND Generation	–	–	–
3RD Generation	–	–	–
4TH Generation	–	$30	$10
5TH Generation	–	–	$10

Gobbles was introduced with four other holiday Beanie Babies* in October 1997. She is the most expensive Beanie Baby* for Ty Inc.* to produce, so don't expect her to last very long as a current.

℞

Goldie was retired on January 1, 1998. Her value has been increasing ever since her retirement. Expect Goldie's price to continue to rise as she becomes harder to find. Goldie shares the same material with orange Digger, Inch, Chocolate's antlers, Pinky's and Caw's bills, and Scoop's and Waddle's bills and feet.

GOLDIE*

The Goldfish ▪ #4023

ESTIMATED PRODUCTION: 1,750,000
STATUS: Retired, 1-1-98
INTRODUCED: 1994 ▪ BIRTHDAY: 11-14-94

HANG TAG	VALUE 7/1/97	VALUE 1/1/98	VALUE 7/1/98
1ST Generation	$75	$175	$550
2ND Generation	$45	$90	$275
3RD Generation	$30	$70	$125
4TH Generation	$10	$20	$50
5TH Generation	–	–	–

GRACIE*

The Swan • #4126

ESTIMATED PRODUCTION: 3,500,000

STATUS: Retired, 5-1-98

INTRODUCED: 1-1-97 • BIRTHDAY: 6-17-96

Gracie was one of the three worst sellers in the Beanie Baby* family last year. It may take some time before she appreciates in value. We expect her new friend Jake the Mallard Duck to be more popular.

HANG TAG	VALUE 7/1/97	VALUE 1/1/98	VALUE 7/1/98
1ST Generation	–	–	–
2ND Generation	–	–	–
3RD Generation	–	–	–
4TH Generation	$10	$10	$20
5TH Generation	–	–	$20

*Trademark or name of Ty, Inc., McDonald's Corporation or other distributors of Ty, Inc. dolls, not affiliated with the authors or Schroeder Publishing.

 **R**

At one time, Grunt was the last Beanie Baby* left on the shelves. He was a horrible seller, so Ty Inc.* retired him. A year later Grunt was selling for around $175. Watch out for all the fake Grunts on the market. They are scrawnier and have horrible tags. Compare it to a Grunt you know is real before buying. See the Counterfeit Section on page 268 of this book.

GRUNT*

The Red Razorback ▪ #4092

ESTIMATED PRODUCTION: 600,000

STATUS: Retired, 5-11-97

INTRODUCED: 1996 ▪ BIRTHDAY: 7-19-95

HANG TAG	VALUE 7/1/97	VALUE 1/1/98	VALUE 7/1/98
1ST Generation	–	–	–
2ND Generation	–	–	–
3RD Generation	$110	$175	$250
4TH Generation	$60	$115	$180
5TH Generation	–	–	–

HAPPY*

The Gray Hippo • #4061

ESTIMATED PRODUCTION: 50,000
STATUS: Retired, 6-3-95
INTRODUCED: 1994 • BIRTHDAY: Unknown

HANG TAG	VALUE 7/1/97	VALUE 1/1/98	VALUE 7/1/98
1ST Generation	$400	$500	$950
2ND Generation	$350	$450	$925
3RD Generation	$300	$400	$900
4TH Generation	–	–	–
5TH Generation	–	–	–

Happy was originally produced with gray material. Happy's value started to rise as people realized how rare he was. Expect Beanie Babies* which have experienced color changes to rise greatly in value, especially gray Happy, orange Digger, and tie-dyed Lizzy.

*Trademark or name of Ty, Inc., McDonald's Corporation or other distributors of Ty, Inc. dolls, not affiliated with the authors or Schroeder Publishing.

Rx

Happy underwent a color change in late 1995. He was originally gray but was changed to the more colorful lavender. He is highly sought after with a third generation tag since it can be switched to a tagless gray Happy.

HAPPY*

The Lavender Hippo ▪ #4061

ESTIMATED PRODUCTION: 3,000,000

STATUS: Retired, 5-1-98

INTRODUCED: 1995 ▪ BIRTHDAY: 2-25-94

HANG TAG	VALUE 7/1/97	VALUE 1/1/98	VALUE 7/1/98
1ST Generation	–	–	–
2ND Generation	–	–	–
3RD Generation	$50	$175	$350
4TH Generation	$10	$10	$30
5TH Generation	–	–	$30

HIPPITY*

The Mint Green Bunny ▪ #4119

ESTIMATED PRODUCTION: 1,500,000
STATUS: Retired, 5-1-98
INTRODUCED: 1-1-97 ▪ BIRTHDAY: 6-1-96

HANG TAG	VALUE 7/1/97	VALUE 1/1/98	VALUE 7/1/98
1ST Generation	–	–	–
2ND Generation	–	–	–
3RD Generation	–	–	–
4TH Generation	$25	$10	$20
5TH Generation	–	–	$20

Hippity was introduced on January 1, 1997, along with Floppity and Hoppity. In 1997, this trio was highly sought after and sold for $75 on the secondary market. Now retired, expect these popular Beanie Babies* to continue to appreciate in value. Hippity was featured in a Fannie May Candy* promotion. See page 247 for details.

R_x

Hissy was a long awaited replacement for Slither. Ty Inc.* decided to coil Hissy which makes him closer to the other Beanie Babies* in size. This is something they did not do for Slither. Hissy's tongue is also attached better than Slither's which often became detached.

HISSY*

The Snake ▪ #4185

ESTIMATED RETIREMENT: 2002
STATUS: Current
INTRODUCED: 1-1-98 ▪ BIRTHDAY: 4-4-97

HANG TAG	VALUE 7/1/97	VALUE 1/1/98	VALUE 7/1/98
1ST Generation	–	–	–
2ND Generation	–	–	–
3RD Generation	–	–	–
4TH Generation	–	–	–
5TH Generation	–	–	$10

*Trademark or name of Ty, Inc., McDonald's Corporation or other distributors of Ty, Inc. dolls, not affiliated with the authors or Schroeder Publishing.

HOOT*

The Owl ▪ #4073

ESTIMATED PRODUCTION: 1,750,000

STATUS: Retired, 10-1-97

INTRODUCED: 1996 ▪ BIRTHDAY: 8-9-95

Hoot was fairly easy to find after his retirement which kept his value under $20. Recently his price has started to climb. Versions of Hoot's poem can be found with "quite" misspelled "qutie." This does not raise the value but makes an interesting addition to your collection.

HANG TAG	VALUE 7/1/97	VALUE 1/1/98	VALUE 7/1/98
1ST Generation	–	–	–
2ND Generation	–	–	–
3RD Generation	$30	$65	$120
4TH Generation	$10	$25	$50
5TH Generation	–	–	–

Since Ty Inc.* retired the Bunny trio; Hoppity, Floppity, and Hippity, we wonder when other bunnies will be introduced. We would love a tie-dyed bunny! Collect all three of the Bunny trio for the best long-term value.

R̲x

HOPPITY*

The Pink Bunny ▪ #4117

ESTIMATED PRODUCTION: 1,500,000
STATUS: Retired, 5-1-98
INTRODUCED: 1-1-97 ▪ BIRTHDAY: 4-3-96

HANG TAG	VALUE 7/1/97	VALUE 1/1/98	VALUE 7/1/98
1ST Generation	–	–	–
2ND Generation	–	–	–
3RD Generation	–	–	–
4TH Generation	$25	$10	$20
5TH Generation	–	–	$20

*Trademark or name of Ty, Inc., McDonald's Corporation or other distributors of Ty, Inc. dolls, not affiliated with the authors or Schroeder Publishing.

71

HUMPHREY*

The Camel ▪ #4060

ESTIMATED PRODUCTION: 20,000

STATUS: Retired, 6-15-95

INTRODUCED: 1994 ▪ BIRTHDAY: Unknown

R

Humphrey was introduced in mid-1994. He was one of the earliest Beanie Babies* to be retired when he called it quits in 1995. He is extremely sought after and is very hard to find with a mint hang tag.

HANG TAG	VALUE 7/1/97	VALUE 1/1/98	VALUE 7/1/98
1ST Generation	$950	$1,500	$2,600
2ND Generation	$900	$1,450	$2,550
3RD Generation	$850	$1,400	$2,500
4TH Generation	–	–	–
5TH Generation	–	–	–

*Trademark or name of Ty, Inc., McDonald's Corporation or other distributors of Ty, Inc. dolls, not affiliated with the authors or Schroeder Publishing.

Rx

Iggy the Iguana and his partner Rainbow the Chameleon have been a puzzle to collectors. When shipments began hitting the store shelves it appeared the tags were switched. Now it appears in actuality the tags were correct but the material was switched. Adding to the confusion, Iggys are now appearing with tongues which appears to be a design change. This should, over time, increase the value of the original Iggy.

IGGY*

The Iguana ▪ #4038
ESTIMATED RETIREMENT: 2000
STATUS: Current
INTRODUCED: 1-1-98 ▪ BIRTHDAY: 8-12-97

HANG TAG	VALUE 7/1/97	VALUE 1/1/98	VALUE 7/1/98
1ST Generation	–	–	–
2ND Generation	–	–	–
3RD Generation	–	–	–
4TH Generation	–	–	–
5TH Generation	–	–	$10

INCH*

The Inchworm with Felt Antennas ■ #4044

ESTIMATED PRODUCTION: 100,000

STATUS: Retired, 1996

INTRODUCED: 1996 ■ BIRTHDAY: Unknown

HANG TAG	VALUE 7/1/97	VALUE 1/1/98	VALUE 7/1/98
1ST Generation	–	–	–
2ND Generation	–	–	–
3RD Generation	$65	$150	$225
4TH Generation	$45	$100	$225
5TH Generation	–	–	–

DR. BEANIE

Rx

The first version of Inch contained antennas that were made out of felt. These were replaced with the current yarn antennas because the felt ones came off easily. This Beanie Baby* is extremely underpriced for its rarity. Look for felt Inch's price to go up considerably.

R̵x

Inch was first produced with felt antennas, but was later changed to the yarn antennas. The blue material on Inch's body is an identical match to the material used for the royal blue Peanut. Kiwi is the only other Beanie Baby* to contain some of this material. Also, the last segment of Inch's body is the same material used for the most recent Patti. Put your older Patti up against Inch to see if you indeed have one of the rare ones.

INCH*

The Inchworm with Yarn Antennas ▪ #4044

ESTIMATED PRODUCTION: 3,750,000

STATUS: Retired, 5-1-98

INTRODUCED: 1996 ▪ BIRTHDAY: 9-3-95

HANG TAG	VALUE 7/1/97	VALUE 1/1/98	VALUE 7/1/98
1ST Generation	–	–	–
2ND Generation	–	–	–
3RD Generation	–	–	–
4TH Generation	$10	$10	$25
5TH Generation	–	–	$25

*Trademark or name of Ty, Inc., McDonald's Corporation or other distributors of Ty, Inc. dolls, not affiliated with the authors or Schroeder Publishing.

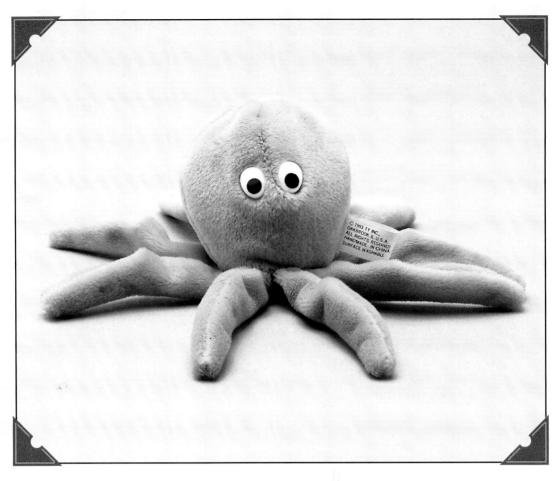

INKY *

The Tan Octopus without a Mouth ▪ #4028

ESTIMATED PRODUCTION: 50,000
STATUS: Retired, 9-12-94
INTRODUCED: 1994 ▪ BIRTHDAY: Unknown

Rx

Inky without a mouth was the first version of Inky produced. This Inky is undervalued and is a great buy at the current secondary market price.

HANG TAG	VALUE 7/1/97	VALUE 1/1/98	VALUE 7/1/98
1ST Generation	$325	$650	$925
2ND Generation	$275	$600	$875
3RD Generation	–	–	–
4TH Generation	–	–	–
5TH Generation	–	–	–

 Dr. BEANIE

Rx

Inky with a mouth was the second version of Inky produced (see Inky without a mouth). He was later changed to a more colorful pink because his tan color was quite drab. Both tan Inky with and without a mouth are great buys due to their rarity.

INKY*

The Tan Octopus with a Mouth ▪ #4028

ESTIMATED PRODUCTION: 100,000

STATUS: Retired, 6-3-95

INTRODUCED: 1994 ▪ BIRTHDAY: Unknown

HANG TAG	VALUE 7/1/97	VALUE 1/1/98	VALUE 7/1/98
1ST Generation	–	–	–
2ND Generation	$275	$500	$825
3RD Generation	$250	$475	$800
4TH Generation	–	–	–
5TH Generation	–	–	–

INKY*

The Pink Octopus ▪ #4028

ESTIMATED PRODUCTION: 3,250,000
STATUS: Retired, 5-1-98
INTRODUCED: 1995 ▪ BIRTHDAY: 11-29-94

HANG TAG	VALUE 7/1/97	VALUE 1/1/98	VALUE 7/1/98
1ST Generation	–	–	–
2ND Generation	–	–	–
3RD Generation	$110	$200	$375
4TH Generation	$10	$10	$35
5TH Generation	–	–	$35

Inky has gone through two style changes. His original color was tan, and he was made with a mouth and without a mouth. He was later changed to pink to get rid of his dull tan look. Many collectors try to get their hands on nine legged and seven legged Inkys which have been sewn incorrectly. These Beanie Babies* fetch over $300 a piece (see the Mistakes and Oddities Section on page 260 of this book).

*Trademark or name of Ty, Inc., McDonald's Corporation or other distributors of Ty, Inc. dolls, not affiliated with the authors or Schroeder Publishing.

Rx

Bird collectors were excited with another colorful bird. Jabber has proven to be a popular new release. Will he be as popular as the colorful retired Kiwi? Time will tell, but we think he is a winner.

JABBER*

The Parrot • #4197

ESTIMATED RETIREMENT: 2000

STATUS: Current

INTRODUCED: 5-30-98 • BIRTHDAY: 10-10-97

HANG TAG	VALUE 7/1/97	VALUE 1/1/98	VALUE 7/1/98
1ST Generation	–	–	–
2ND Generation	–	–	–
3RD Generation	–	–	–
4TH Generation	–	–	–
5TH Generation	–	–	$20

JAKE *

The Mallard Duck ▪ #4199

ESTIMATED RETIREMENT: 2002

STATUS: Current

INTRODUCED: 5-30-98 ▪ BIRTHDAY: 4-16-97

Jake the drake was announced prematurely when he was shown on several websites two weeks before the official announcement. Jake was one of the first new releases to be shipped. Jake's head contains the same fabric as the jade Teddy.

HANG TAG	VALUE 7/1/97	VALUE 1/1/98	VALUE 7/1/98
1ST Generation	–	–	–
2ND Generation	–	–	–
3RD Generation	–	–	–
4TH Generation	–	–	–
5TH Generation	–	–	$30

Rx

Jolly was a replacement for the earlier retired Tusk. He doesn't lie on his stomach like Tusk. Unlike Tusk, Jolly has a bushy mustache. His tusks are filled in, not just a piece of felt like Tusk's.

JOLLY*

The Walrus ▪ #4082

ESTIMATED PRODUCTION: 1,250,000
STATUS: Retired, 5-1-98
INTRODUCED: 5-11-97 ▪ BIRTHDAY: 12-2-96

HANG TAG	VALUE 7/1/97	VALUE 1/1/98	VALUE 7/1/98
1ST Generation	–	–	–
2ND Generation	–	–	–
3RD Generation	–	–	–
4TH Generation	$10	$10	$25
5TH Generation	–	–	$25

*Trademark or name of Ty, Inc., McDonald's Corporation or other distributors of Ty, Inc. dolls, not affiliated with the authors or Schroeder Publishing.

The Toucan ▪ #4070

ESTIMATED PRODUCTION: 600,000

STATUS: Retired, 1-1-97

INTRODUCED: 1995 ▪ BIRTHDAY: 9-16-95

 **R**x

Kiwi has a similar body style to Caw's. Kiwi shares royal blue Peanut's fabric. Many counterfeit Kiwis are circulating. See the Counterfeit Section on page 268 in this book for more Kiwi information.

HANG TAG	VALUE 7/1/97	VALUE 1/1/98	VALUE 7/1/98
1ST Generation	–	–	–
2ND Generation	–	–	–
3RD Generation	$85	$165	$300
4TH Generation	$50	$120	$210
5TH Generation	–	–	–

BEANIE DR.

R_{X}

Kuku was one of the six birds introduced on the same day, May 30, 1998. Ty Inc.* is always full of surprises and collectors wondered why there would be six new birds at the same time. Collectors agree Ty Inc.'s* unpredictable actions are part of his marketing success.

KUKU *

The Cockatoo ▪ #4192

ESTIMATED RETIREMENT: 2001

STATUS: Current

INTRODUCED: 5-30-98 ▪ BIRTHDAY: 1-5-97

HANG TAG	VALUE 7/1/97	VALUE 1/1/98	VALUE 7/1/98
1ST Generation	–	–	–
2ND Generation	–	–	–
3RD Generation	–	–	–
4TH Generation	–	–	–
5TH Generation	–	–	$20

*Trademark or name of Ty, Inc., McDonald's Corporation or other distributors of Ty, Inc. dolls, not affiliated with the authors or Schroeder Publishing.

83

LEFTY *

The Donkey ▪ #4057

ESTIMATED PRODUCTION: 250,000

STATUS: Retired, 1-1-97

INTRODUCED: 1996 ▪ BIRTHDAY: 7-4-96

HANG TAG	VALUE 7/1/97	VALUE 1/1/98	VALUE 7/1/98
1ST Generation	–	–	–
2ND Generation	–	–	–
3RD Generation	–	–	–
4TH Generation	$60	$150	$300
5TH Generation	–	–	–

*Trademark or name of Ty, Inc., McDonald's Corporation or other distributors of Ty, Inc. dolls, not affiliated with the authors or Schroeder Publishing.

DR. BEANIE

Rx

Lefty, along with the other American trio members are great sellers. They also make up the three most valuable January 1997 retirees. These Beanie Babies* skyrocketed in value in late 1997 and early 1998, when they tripled in value within two months. Now they have settled in price but are still good sellers. The donkey is the symbol of the Democratic Party.

Legs is the least popular and cheapest of the October retirees. Legs was found in retail stores long after he was retired. Because of this, his value was very low. Recently Legs' value has risen some and expect it to rise even more as his availability decreases. See page 266 in the Counterfeit Section for a picture of a fake Legs.

LEGS*

The Frog ▪ #4020

ESTIMATED PRODUCTION: 2,500,000
STATUS: Retired, 10-1-97
INTRODUCED: 1994 ▪ BIRTHDAY: 4-25-93

HANG TAG	VALUE 7/1/97	VALUE 1/1/98	VALUE 7/1/98
1ST Generation	–	$140	$325
2ND Generation	–	$115	$240
3RD Generation	$20	$55	$110
4TH Generation	$10	$15	$30
5TH Generation	–	–	–

*Trademark or name of Ty, Inc., McDonald's Corporation or other distributors of Ty, Inc. dolls, not affiliated with the authors or Schroeder Publishing.

LIBEARTY *

The Bear ▪ #4057

ESTIMATED PRODUCTION: 150,000

STATUS: Retired, 1-1-97

INTRODUCED: 6-15-96 ▪ BIRTHDAY: Summer 1996

 DR. BEANIE

R𝒙

Libearty is the most valuable of the American trio (Lefty, Righty, and Libearty). He was made to commemorate the 1996 Olympics in Atlanta. He is the only Beanie Baby* with a fourth generation hang tag that does not have a birthday listed. Some Libeartys can be found with a hang tag that has Ty Inc.'s* website address cut off. This tag is worth just as much as a normal Libearty tag. The first Libeartys to be produced had clear tag fasteners and the word "Beanie" on the tush tag was misspelled as "Beanine."

HANG TAG	VALUE 7/1/97	VALUE 1/1/98	VALUE 7/1/98
1ST Generation	–	–	–
2ND Generation	–	–	–
3RD Generation	–	–	–
4TH Generation	$75	$175	$400
5TH Generation	–	–	–

*Trademark or name of Ty, Inc., McDonald's Corporation or other distributors of Ty, Inc. dolls, not affiliated with the authors or Schroeder Publishing.

 **R**x

Tie-dyed Lizzy is the first version of the blue and black Lizzy. She is extremely rare and is one of the best buys at current market value. No one really realizes how rare Lizzy is. Expect her value to escalate dramatically in the near future. Many played-with Lizzys have the tongue missing which decreases the value by 75%.

LIZZY*

The Tie-Dyed Lizard ▪ #4033

ESTIMATED PRODUCTION: 10,000
STATUS: Retired, 1-7-96
INTRODUCED: 1995 ▪ BIRTHDAY: Unknown

HANG TAG	VALUE 7/1/97	VALUE 1/1/98	VALUE 7/1/98
1ST Generation	–	–	–
2ND Generation	–	–	–
3RD Generation	$375	$600	$1,400
4TH Generation	–	–	–
5TH Generation	–	–	–

LIZZY*

The Blue Lizard ▪ #4033

ESTIMATED PRODUCTION: 2,500,000
STATUS: Retired, 1-1-98
INTRODUCED: 1996 ▪ BIRTHDAY: 5-11-95

Rx

Lizzy the blue Lizard was a color change for the old tie-dyed Lizzy. Third generation tagged Lizzys are selling for a high price as the hang tag can be switched to a tagless tie-dyed Lizzy.

HANG TAG	VALUE 7/1/97	VALUE 1/1/98	VALUE 7/1/98
1ST Generation	–	–	–
2ND Generation	–	–	–
3RD Generation	$50	$150	$425
4TH Generation	$10	$20	$30
5TH Generation	–	–	$35

*Trademark or name of Ty, Inc., McDonald's Corporation or other distributors of Ty, Inc. dolls, not affiliated with the authors or Schroeder Publishing.

 **R** BEANIE DR.

"Seven spot Lucky" as she is often referred to, was the first version of Lucky produced. It was found that her glued-on felt spots easily came off. Because of this a new 11 spot fabric with printed spots replaced the old fabric. See 11 Spot Lucky.

LUCKY*

The Ladybug with 7 Glued on Spots ▪ #4040

ESTIMATED PRODUCTION: 75,000

STATUS: Retired, 2-27-96

INTRODUCED: 1994 ▪ BIRTHDAY: Unknown

HANG TAG	VALUE 7/1/97	VALUE 1/1/98	VALUE 7/1/98
1ST Generation	$110	$180	$475
2ND Generation	$85	$150	$350
3RD Generation	$60	$120	$250
4TH Generation	–	–	–
5TH Generation	–	–	–

LUCKY*

The Ladybug with 21 Spots ▪ #4040

ESTIMATED PRODUCTION: 25,000
STATUS: Retired, 1996
INTRODUCED: 1996 ▪ BIRTHDAY: 5-1-95

HANG TAG	VALUE 7/1/97	VALUE 1/1/98	VALUE 7/1/98
1ST Generation	–	–	–
2ND Generation	–	–	–
3RD Generation	–	–	–
4TH Generation	–	$450	$800
5TH Generation	–	–	–

R℞

Though "21 spot Lucky" is the third Lucky to be produced, she is the most valuable. The case with most Beanie Babies* is the older the more valuable. This is not true with Lucky. Twenty-one spot Lucky replaced the 11 spot Lucky for a couple months in mid-1996. Many people started buying the 11 spot Lucky, thinking it was a permanent change. They were fooled however, and the 11 spot Lucky soon replaced the hard-to-find 21 spot Lucky.

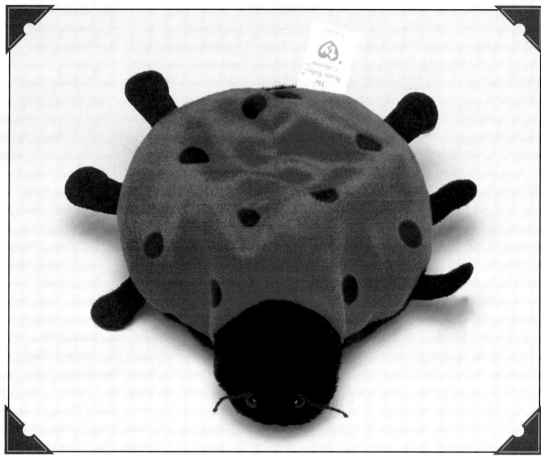

Lucky has gone through three style changes in her life. First produced with 7 felt spots, she was then changed to the current 11 spot form. Lucky was then produced for a short time with 21 spots before being changed back to her 11 spot form. Lucky was part of a spring 1998 Fannie May* promotion. See the Promotion Section on page 247 of this book for more details.

LUCKY*

The Ladybug with 11 Spots ▪ #4040

ESTIMATED PRODUCTION: 2,500,000

STATUS: Retired, 5-1-98

INTRODUCED: 1996 ▪ BIRTHDAY: 5-1-95

HANG TAG	VALUE 7/1/97	VALUE 1/1/98	VALUE 7/1/98
1ST Generation	–	–	–
2ND Generation	–	–	–
3RD Generation	–	–	–
4TH Generation	$10	$10	$35
5TH Generation	–	–	$35

*Trademark or name of Ty, Inc., McDonald's Corporation or other distributors of Ty, Inc. dolls, not affiliated with the authors or Schroeder Publishing.

91

MAGIC*

The Dragon with Hot Pink Stitching ▪ #4088

ESTIMATED PRODUCTION: 75,000

STATUS: Retired, 1996

INTRODUCED: Summer 1996 ▪ BIRTHDAY: 9-5-95

HANG TAG	VALUE 7/1/97	VALUE 1/1/98	VALUE 7/1/98
1ST Generation	–	–	–
2ND Generation	–	–	–
3RD Generation	$95	$150	$225
4TH Generation	–	–	–
5TH Generation	–	–	–

In the summer of 1996, the color of the stitching in Magic's wings changed from light pink to hot pink. This change was only present for about two months before the stitching was changed back to the original color. This shows how Beanie Baby* collectors pay attention to every little detail.

*Trademark or name of Ty, Inc., McDonald's Corporation or other distributors of Ty, Inc. dolls, not affiliated with the authors or Schroeder Publishing.

Rx

Magic was never plentiful while current so expect Magic to continue to go up in value as supplies of her run out. Note, for a short period in 1996 a version of Magic was produced with hot pink stitching (see previous page).

MAGIC *

The Dragon with the Light Pink Stitching ▪ #4088

ESTIMATED PRODUCTION: 2,000,000
STATUS: Retired, 1-1-98
INTRODUCED: 1995 ▪ BIRTHDAY: 9-5-95

HANG TAG	VALUE 7/1/97	VALUE 1/1/98	VALUE 7/1/98
1ST Generation	–	–	–
2ND Generation	–	–	–
3RD Generation	$45	$85	$135
4TH Generation	$18	$25	$55
5TH Generation	–	–	–

*Trademark or name of Ty, Inc., McDonald's Corporation or other distributors of Ty, Inc. dolls, not affiliated with the authors or Schroeder Publishing.

MANNY *

The Manatee ▪ #4081

ESTIMATED PRODUCTION: 600,000
STATUS: Retired, 5-11-97
INTRODUCED: 1996 ▪ BIRTHDAY: 6-8-95

HANG TAG	VALUE 7/1/97	VALUE 1/1/98	VALUE 7/1/98
1ST Generation	–	–	–
2ND Generation	–	–	–
3RD Generation	$90	$155	$280
4TH Generation	$50	$120	$215
5TH Generation	–	–	–

Manny was not a great seller when she was a current. This is probably because she has a pretty dull appearance. After retiring, Manny quickly went up in value. Manny was always most popular in Florida, where manatees can be found, but is now popular with all Beanie Baby* collectors.

DR. BEANIE

R

Maple is a Canadian exclusive Beanie Baby*. Even though he is a current Beanie Baby*, Maple is nearly impossible to find in a retail store in Canada. Because of this, Maple's price has escalated and he is especially sought after in places other than Canada. One reason why Maple's price has gone up so much is because Customs has not been letting Maples cross the border to the United States.

MAPLE*

The Canadian Bear ▪ #4600

ESTIMATED RETIREMENT: 1999

STATUS: Current

INTRODUCED: 1997 ▪ BIRTHDAY: 7-1-96

HANG TAG	VALUE 7/1/97	VALUE 1/1/98	VALUE 7/1/98
1ST Generation	–	–	–
2ND Generation	–	–	–
3RD Generation	–	–	–
4TH Generation	$80	$125	$325
5TH Generation	–	–	$325

MAPLE[*]
SPECIAL OLYMPICS

The Canadian Bear ▪ #4600

ESTIMATED PRODUCTION: 10,000
STATUS: Retired, 1997

INTRODUCED: 8-97 ▪ BIRTHDAY: 7-1-96

HANG TAG	VALUE 7/1/97	VALUE 1/1/98	VALUE 7/1/98
1ST Generation	–	–	–
2ND Generation	–	–	–
3RD Generation	–	–	–
4TH Generation	$225	$350	$750
5TH Generation	–	–	–

*Trademark or name of Ty, Inc., McDonald's Corporation or other distributors of Ty, Inc. dolls, not affiliated with the authors or Schroeder Publishing.

DR. BEANIE   R_x

The Special Olympics Maple was given out to about 10,000 people who attended the 1997 Special Olympics. It has an extra Special Olympics Sports Festival tag that is usually attached to the same ear as the hang tag. Don't be worried if your Sports Festival tag is not connected through the perforation in the tag. Because many of them were ripping off, most tag connectors were just forced through the tag elsewhere, creating its own hole.

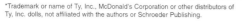

R̸

The first 3,000 Maples produced had the tush tag name of Pride. This was an error which Ty Inc.* then corrected. Maple-Prides have a Maple hang tag.

MAPLE*
PRIDE

The Canadian Bear ▪ #4600
ESTIMATED PRODUCTION: 3,000
STATUS: Retired, 1997
INTRODUCED: 1997 ▪ BIRTHDAY: 7-1-96

Tush Tag

HANG TAG	VALUE 7/1/97	VALUE 1/1/98	VALUE 7/1/98
1ST Generation	–	–	–
2ND Generation	–	–	–
3RD Generation	–	–	–
4TH Generation	$220	$480	$900
5TH Generation	–	–	–

MEL*

The Koala ▪ #4162

ESTIMATED RETIREMENT: 2002

STATUS: Current

INTRODUCED: 1-1-97 ▪ BIRTHDAY: 1-15-96

HANG TAG	VALUE 7/1/97	VALUE 1/1/98	VALUE 7/1/98
1ST Generation	–	–	–
2ND Generation	–	–	–
3RD Generation	–	–	–
4TH Generation	$10	$10	$10
5TH Generation	–	–	$10

Mel is rumored to be named after the actor Mel Gibson. (Read the last line of his poem.) Mel is one of the rarer currents, however, he never seems to be mentioned when talking about hard to finds. People will realize the extent of his rareness once he is retired and everybody wants to get their hands on him.

Fine-mane Mystic is the first version of Mystic produced. She contains the same type of yarn that fine-mane Derby has. This fine yarn was changed to a coarse yarn because it became easily unraveled. Mystic is a little more plentiful than fine-mane Derby, but is not an easy one to come across. Mystic is a great buy at current market value and should increase in value considerably as more people learn of her existence.

R

MYSTIC*

The Fine-Mane Unicorn ▪ #4007

ESTIMATED PRODUCTION: 30,000

STATUS: Retired, 1995

INTRODUCED: 1994 ▪ BIRTHDAY: Unknown

HANG TAG	VALUE 7/1/97	VALUE 1/1/98	VALUE 7/1/98
1ST Generation	$160	$250	$650
2ND Generation	$125	$225	$600
3RD Generation	$90	$200	$550
4TH Generation	–	–	–
5TH Generation	–	–	–

MYSTIC *

The Coarse-Mane Unicorn ▪ #4007

ESTIMATED PRODUCTION: 3,000,000

STATUS: Retired, 10-23-97

INTRODUCED: 1996 ▪ BIRTHDAY: 5-21-94

DR. BEANIE

Rx

Coarse-mane Mystic is the second version of Mystic produced (see fine-mane Mystic). She was officially retired by Ty Inc.* late in October 1997 and replaced with an iridescent horned Beanie Baby*.

HANG TAG	VALUE 7/1/97	VALUE 1/1/98	VALUE 7/1/98
1ST Generation	–	–	–
2ND Generation	–	–	–
3RD Generation	$25	$40	$200
4TH Generation	$10	$10	$20
5TH Generation	–	–	–

*Trademark or name of Ty, Inc., McDonald's Corporation or other distributors of Ty, Inc. dolls, not affiliated with the authors or Schroeder Publishing.

R̥

This new iridescent-horned Mystic is actually the third Mystic that has been made. The first was the fine-mane Mystic followed by the coarse-mane tan horn Mystic. The iridescent Mystic was selling for $20 - $25 when she first came into the market, but that price drops each time she becomes more available.

MYSTIC *

The Coarse-Mane Unicorn with Iridescent Horn ▪ #4007

ESTIMATED RETIREMENT: 1999

STATUS: Current

INTRODUCED: 1997 ▪ BIRTHDAY: 5-21-94

HANG TAG	VALUE 7/1/97	VALUE 1/1/98	VALUE 7/1/98
1ST Generation	–	–	–
2ND Generation	–	–	–
3RD Generation	–	–	–
4TH Generation	–	$10	$10
5TH Generation	–	–	$10

*Trademark or name of Ty, Inc., McDonald's Corporation or other distributors of Ty, Inc. dolls, not affiliated with the authors or Schroeder Publishing.

NANA *

The Monkey ▪ #4067
ESTIMATED PRODUCTION: 1,500
STATUS: Retired, 1995
INTRODUCED: 1995 ▪ BIRTHDAY: Unknown

The Beanie Babies ™ Collection
© Ty Inc.
Oakbrook IL. U.S.A.
Ty UK Ltd.
Waterlooville, Hants
PO8 8HH
Ty Deutschland
90008 Nürnberg
Handmade in China

Nana ™ style 4067
to _____
from _____
with
love

HANG TAG	VALUE 7/1/97	VALUE 1/1/98	VALUE 7/1/98
1ST Generation	–	–	–
2ND Generation	–	–	–
3RD Generation	$1,200	$3,000	$5,200
4TH Generation	–	–	–
5TH Generation	–	–	–

DR. BEANIE

℞

Nana was the first name of Bongo. Very few (only 1,500) Nanas were produced. He is a true prize for collectors. Very few mint Nana tags have been found. Many of the 1,500 that were produced are now probably tagless. Because of this, collectors will pay whatever they have to just to get a hold of a Nana even if the tag can barely be read. Most Nanas' hang tags contained Bongo stickers covering the name Nana. Only the very first ones were stickerless. These first Nanas command top dollar.

*Trademark or name of Ty, Inc., McDonald's Corporation or other distributors of Ty, Inc. dolls, not affiliated with the authors or Schroeder Publishing.

 **Dr. BEANIE** **R**x

Nanook is one of the harder to find currents and is rarely left on the shelves. A favorite in Alaska and Canada, Nanook was used as a promotion for the Yukon Quest Dog Sled Race. See the Promotions Section on page 245 of this book for more information.

NANOOK*

The Husky ▪ #4104

ESTIMATED RETIREMENT: 2000
STATUS: Current
INTRODUCED: 5-11-97 ▪ BIRTHDAY: 11-21-96

HANG TAG	VALUE 7/1/97	VALUE 1/1/98	VALUE 7/1/98
1ST Generation	–	–	–
2ND Generation	–	–	–
3RD Generation	–	–	–
4TH Generation	$10	$10	$10
5TH Generation	–	–	$10

NIP*

The Gold Cat with White Face and Belly ▪ #4003

ESTIMATED PRODUCTION: 2,500,000
STATUS: Retired, 1-7-96
INTRODUCED: 1995 ▪ BIRTHDAY: Unknown

Rx

Nip the gold cat with white face and belly is larger than the Nips which follow him. Many collectors consider him a kitten. He is the same size as Zip with a white belly and face.

HANG TAG	VALUE 7/1/97	VALUE 1/1/98	VALUE 7/1/98
1ST Generation	–	–	–
2ND Generation	$200	$375	$550
3RD Generation	$175	$350	$525
4TH Generation	–	–	–
5TH Generation	–	–	–

*Trademark or name of Ty, Inc., McDonald's Corporation or other distributors of Ty, Inc. dolls, not affiliated with the authors or Schroeder Publishing.

Rx

The all gold Nip was the second version of Nip made. He is smaller than the previous Nip. Since fewer all gold Nips were made he has the highest value.

NIP *

The All Gold Cat ▪ #4003

ESTIMATED PRODUCTION: 15,000
STATUS: Retired, 3-10-96
INTRODUCED: 1996 ▪ BIRTHDAY: Unknown

HANG TAG	VALUE 7/1/97	VALUE 1/1/98	VALUE 7/1/98
1ST Generation	–	–	–
2ND Generation	–	–	–
3RD Generation	$425	$750	$1,200
4TH Generation	–	–	–
5TH Generation	–	–	–

NIP*

The Gold Cat with White Paws ▪ #4003

ESTIMATED PRODUCTION: 60,000
STATUS: Retired, 1-1-98
INTRODUCED: 1996 ▪ BIRTHDAY: 3-6-94

Dr. BEANIE — Rx

Nip has had three style changes. This white pawed Nip is the third and final version. Nip is part of the "ip" family of cats: Nip, Zip, Snip, Chip, and Flip.

HANG TAG	VALUE 7/1/97	VALUE 1/1/98	VALUE 7/1/98
1ST Generation	–	–	–
2ND Generation	–	–	–
3RD Generation	$80	$200	$425
4TH Generation	$10	$10	$25
5TH Generation	–	–	$30

 **BEANIE DR.**

R_x

Nuts is one of the average selling currents. He is not hard to find, but usually isn't one of the last Beanie Babies* left on the shelves. Don't expect Nuts to be retired until a few years down the road.

NUTS*

The Squirrel ▪ #4114

ESTIMATED RETIREMENT: 2003
STATUS: Current
INTRODUCED: 1-1-97 ▪ BIRTHDAY: 1-21-96

HANG TAG	VALUE 7/1/97	VALUE 1/1/98	VALUE 7/1/98
1ST Generation	–	–	–
2ND Generation	–	–	–
3RD Generation	–	–	–
4TH Generation	$10	$10	$10
5TH Generation	–	–	$10

*Trademark or name of Ty, Inc., McDonald's Corporation or other distributors of Ty, Inc. dolls, not affiliated with the authors or Schroeder Publishing.

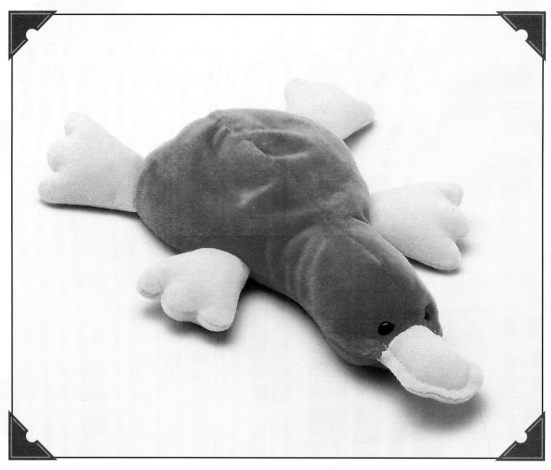

PATTI*

The Deep Fuchsia Platypus ▪ #4025
ESTIMATED PRODUCTION: 10,000
STATUS: Retired, 1993
INTRODUCED: 1993 ▪ BIRTHDAY: Unknown

R

Deep fuchsia Patti was the first version of Patti produced. This Patti was one of the three Beanie Babies* produced before the original nine came out. The others were Punchers and Brownie. Some consider these pre-original nine Beanie Baby* prototypes, but we, as serious collectors, consider them as part of the regular set. This Patti only comes with a 1st or 2nd generation hang tag and was produced in Korea.

HANG TAG	VALUE 7/1/97	VALUE 1/1/98	VALUE 7/1/98
1ST Generation	$650	$850	$1,500
2ND Generation	$600	$850	$1,400
3RD Generation	–	–	–
4TH Generation	–	–	–
5TH Generation	–	–	–

*Trademark or name of Ty, Inc., McDonald's Corporation or other distributors of Ty, Inc. dolls, not affiliated with the authors or Schroeder Publishing.

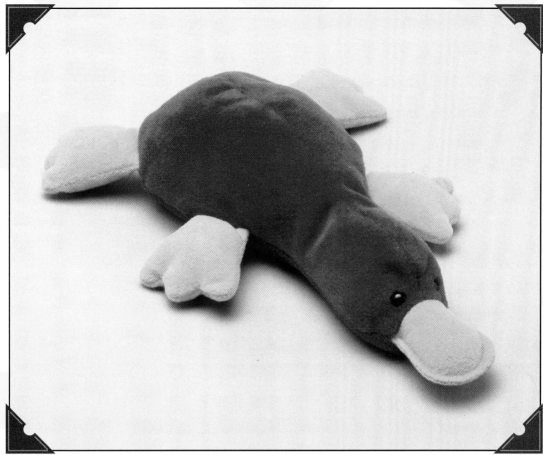

 **BEANIE**
DR.

R$_x$

Raspberry Patti was one of the original nine Beanie Babies* produced. These Pattis come with a 1st or 2nd generation hang tag, and a black and white 1993 tush tag that was made in Korea. Her bill has more of a rounded shape compared to the other Pattis.

PATTI*

The Raspberry Platypus ▪ #4025

ESTIMATED PRODUCTION: 20,000

STATUS: Retired

INTRODUCED: 1993 ▪ BIRTHDAY: Unknown

HANG TAG	VALUE 7/1/97	VALUE 1/1/98	VALUE 7/1/98
1ST Generation	$325	$750	$1,000
2ND Generation	$300	$700	$1,100
3RD Generation	–	–	–
4TH Generation	–	–	–
5TH Generation	–	–	–

*Trademark or name of Ty, Inc., McDonald's Corporation or other distributors of Ty, Inc. dolls, not affiliated with the authors or Schroeder Publishing.

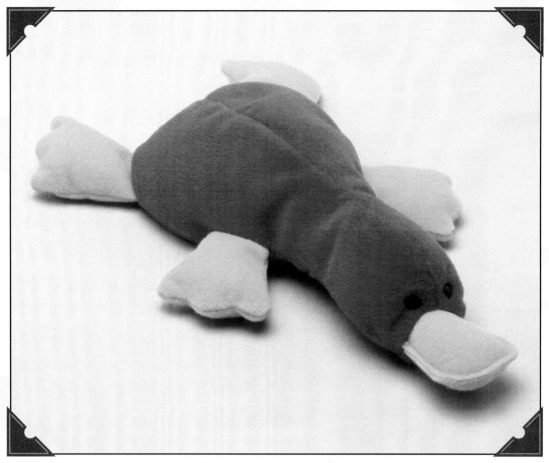

PATTI *

The Magenta Platypus ▪ #4025

ESTIMATED PRODUCTION: 30,000
STATUS: Retired, 1995
INTRODUCED: 1993 ▪ BIRTHDAY: Unknown

HANG TAG	VALUE 7/1/97	VALUE 1/1/98	VALUE 7/1/98
1ST Generation	–	–	–
2ND Generation	–	–	–
3RD Generation	$225	$600	$1,000
4TH Generation	–	–	–
5TH Generation	–	–	–

*Trademark or name of Ty, Inc., McDonald's Corporation or other distributors of Ty, Inc. dolls, not affiliated with the authors or Schroeder Publishing.

R⤬

Magenta Patti was the third version of Patti produced. These Pattis come with 3rd generation hang tags and were made in China. The color of raspberry Patti and magenta Patti is nearly identical. The best way to tell the difference is by looking where the Beanie Baby* was made on the tush tag. Also, the magenta Patti has a more square shaped bill than the raspberry Patti.

 **Dr. BEANIE**

Rx

The fuchsia Patti was the fourth version of Patti. All four have nearly the same body style. The colors are slightly different. To verify if you have this fuchsia Patti compare the fabric to the purple on Inch. It should match exactly.

PATTI*

The Fuchsia Platypus ▪ #4025

ESTIMATED PRODUCTION: 1,750,000

STATUS: Retired, 5-1-98

INTRODUCED: 1993 ▪ BIRTHDAY: 1-6-93

HANG TAG	VALUE 7/1/97	VALUE 1/1/98	VALUE 7/1/98
1ST Generation	–	–	–
2ND Generation	–	–	–
3RD Generation	$90	$200	$450
4TH Generation	$10	$25	$25
5TH Generation	–	–	$25

*Trademark or name of Ty, Inc., McDonald's Corporation or other distributors of Ty, Inc. dolls, not affiliated with the authors or Schroeder Publishing.

PEACE*

The Tie-Dyed Teddy ▪ #4053

ESTIMATED RETIREMENT: 1998
STATUS: Current
INTRODUCED: 5-11-97 ▪ BIRTHDAY: 2-1-96

HANG TAG	VALUE 7/1/97	VALUE 1/1/98	VALUE 7/1/98
1ST Generation	–	–	–
2ND Generation	–	–	–
3RD Generation	–	–	–
4TH Generation	$100	$75	$35
5TH Generation	–	–	$35

Peace is rumored to have been a replacement for Garcia because of a threatened lawsuit from Jerry Garcia's estate. Peace is one of the hardest currents to find. Last summer Peace was selling for around $100. His price dropped substantially once he became a little more available. Expect his price to go up considerably once he is retired.

 **BEANIE** **Rx**

The royal blue Peanut is the "jewel" of the Beanie Baby* family. It is not the rarest Beanie Baby*, but it is the most popular. Owning this Peanut is every Beanie Baby* collector's dream. Not many of these dreams can be fulfilled since only around 2,000 were made. Royal blue Peanut was actually a mistake. It was distributed in June 1996 but Ty Inc.* quickly corrected the material to the light blue that was originally intended for Peanut.

PEANUT*

The Royal Blue Elephant ▪ #4062

ESTIMATED PRODUCTION: 2,000
STATUS: Retired, 10-2-95
INTRODUCED: 1995 ▪ BIRTHDAY: Unknown

HANG TAG	VALUE 7/1/97	VALUE 1/1/98	VALUE 7/1/98
1ST Generation	–	–	–
2ND Generation	–	–	–
3RD Generation	$1,400	$3,000	$5,500
4TH Generation	–	–	–
5TH Generation	–	–	–

PEANUT[*]

The Light Blue Elephant ▪ #4062
ESTIMATED PRODUCTION: 3,000,000
STATUS: Retired, 5-1-98
INTRODUCED: 1995 ▪ BIRTHDAY: 1-25-95

DR. BEANIE

Rx

The light blue Peanut is the second version of the elephant. For a month in 1995, Peanut was produced as royal blue Peanut. This royal blue Peanut was quickly changed to the light blue color that she is today. The 3rd generation tagged light blue Peanut is extremely sought after in mint condition. This 3rd generation tag can be switched to a tagless royal blue Peanut.

HANG TAG	VALUE 7/1/97	VALUE 1/1/98	VALUE 7/1/98
1ST Generation	–	–	–
2ND Generation	–	–	–
3RD Generation	$250	$700	$1,750
4TH Generation	$10	$10	$30
5TH Generation	–	–	$30

*Trademark or name of Ty, Inc., McDonald's Corporation or other distributors of Ty, Inc. dolls, not affiliated with the authors or Schroeder Publishing.

 **Rx**

Peking was introduced in mid-1994 and was retired in 1995. Not many Pekings were made. It is difficult to find Peking (or Chilly) in perfect condition. Most Pekings' stomachs are not nearly as white as originally. Beware of counterfeit Pekings. These fakes are scrawnier and the face is shaped differently. The nose comes to more of a point. The hang tag on most fakes left off the two dots on the top of the German ü. See page 267 for a picture of a counterfeit Peking.

PEKING*

The Panda ▪ #4013

ESTIMATED PRODUCTION: 25,000

STATUS: Retired, 1-7-96

INTRODUCED: 1994 ▪ BIRTHDAY: Unknown

HANG TAG	VALUE 7/1/97	VALUE 1/1/98	VALUE 7/1/98
1ST Generation	$375	$1,100	$2,500
2ND Generation	$350	$1,050	$2,500
3RD Generation	$300	$1,000	$2,500
4TH Generation	–	–	–
5TH Generation	–	–	–

*Trademark or name of Ty, Inc., McDonald's Corporation or other distributors of Ty, Inc. dolls, not affiliated with the authors or Schroeder Publishing.

PINCHERS *

The Lobster ▪ #4026

ESTIMATED PRODUCTION: 4,000,000

STATUS: Retired, 5-1-98

INTRODUCED: 1994 ▪ BIRTHDAY: 6-19-93

DR. BEANIE

Rx

Pinchers is actually Punchers with a name change and slight body modification. There is little difference between the two (see Punchers). Pinchers is one of the original nine and is highly sought after with a first generation tag.

HANG TAG	VALUE 7/1/97	VALUE 1/1/98	VALUE 7/1/98
1ST Generation	$100	$140	$390
2ND Generation	$60	$120	$280
3RD Generation	$30	$60	$110
4TH Generation	$10	$10	$20
5TH Generation	–	–	$20

*Trademark or name of Ty, Inc., McDonald's Corporation or other distributors of Ty, Inc. dolls, not affiliated with the authors or Schroeder Publishing.

BEANIE
DR.

Rx

Pinky is one of the hardest to find currents and the most difficult Teenie Beanie* to find. Expect this pink flamingo to retire soon. Many people were talking about a red Pinky in late 1997. No one was really sure of its origin. See page 269 of this book for red Pinky pictures.

PINKY *

The Flamingo ▪ #4072

ESTIMATED RETIREMENT: 1999
STATUS: Current
INTRODUCED: 1995 ▪ BIRTHDAY: 2-13-95

HANG TAG	VALUE 7/1/97	VALUE 1/1/98	VALUE 7/1/98
1ST Generation	–	–	–
2ND Generation	–	–	–
3RD Generation	$35	$45	$100
4TH Generation	$20	$10	$10
5TH Generation	–	–	$10

POUCH*

The Kangaroo ▪ #4161

ESTIMATED RETIREMENT: 1999

STATUS: Current

INTRODUCED: 1-1-97 ▪ BIRTHDAY: 11-6-96

HANG TAG	VALUE 7/1/97	VALUE 1/1/98	VALUE 7/1/98
1ST Generation	–	–	–
2ND Generation	–	–	–
3RD Generation	–	–	–
4TH Generation	$10	$10	$10
5TH Generation	–	–	$10

Pouch is relatively easy to find. Look for her to possibly retire because her baby could be a child safety hazard. Either a retirement or style change is definitely in the near future.

*Trademark or name of Ty, Inc., McDonald's Corporation or other distributors of Ty, Inc. dolls, not affiliated with the authors or Schroeder Publishing.

 **Rx**

Beanie Baby* collectors love cats. Pounce immediately was a popular new 1998 Beanie Baby*. Currently, there are seven Beanie Baby* cats (not counting style changes).

POUNCE*

The Brown Cat ▪ #4122

ESTIMATED RETIREMENT: 2002
STATUS: Current
INTRODUCED: 1-1-98 ▪ BIRTHDAY: 8-28-97

HANG TAG	VALUE 7/1/97	VALUE 1/1/98	VALUE 7/1/98
1ST Generation	–	–	–
2ND Generation	–	–	–
3RD Generation	–	–	–
4TH Generation	–	–	$10
5TH Generation	–	–	$10

*Trademark or name of Ty, Inc., McDonald's Corporation or other distributors of Ty, Inc. dolls, not affiliated with the authors or Schroeder Publishing.

119

PRANCE *

The Gray Cat ▪ #4123

ESTIMATED RETIREMENT: 2002
STATUS: Current
INTRODUCED: 1-1-98 ▪ BIRTHDAY: 11-20-97

HANG TAG	VALUE 7/1/97	VALUE 1/1/98	VALUE 7/1/98
1ST Generation	–	–	–
2ND Generation	–	–	–
3RD Generation	–	–	–
4TH Generation	–	$15	$10
5TH Generation	–	–	$10

Prance and Pounce caused some confusion when first released in January 1998. Some dealers felt Prance's and Pounce's tags were reversed. This was caused by a misprint in a major Beanie Baby* magazine and was proved not to be true.

Rx

Princess the Bear, was released to benefit the Diana, Princess of Wales, Fund. In December 1997 each Ty Inc.* dealer was allotted 12 Princess Bears. In early 1998, Princess was released once again with a small tag change. The tush tag now read "P.E." pellets instead of "P.V.C." pellets. These P.E. pellet Princesses sell for about $100 less than the original Princess. See the Special Promotions Section on page 248 of this book for more information. Also see page 266 for a picture of a counterfeit Princess.

PRINCESS*

The Bear ▪ #4300

ESTIMATED RETIREMENT: 1999
STATUS: Current
INTRODUCED: 10-29-97 ▪ BIRTHDAY: Unknown

HANG TAG	VALUE 7/1/97	VALUE 1/1/98	VALUE 7/1/98
1ST Generation	–	–	–
2ND Generation	–	–	–
3RD Generation	–	–	–
4TH Generation	P.V.C.	$400	$150
	P.E.	–	$50
5TH Generation	–	–	–

PUFFER *

The Puffin ▪ #4185

ESTIMATED RETIREMENT: 2001
STATUS: Current
INTRODUCED: 1-1-98 ▪ BIRTHDAY: 11-3-97

Rx

Puffer the Puffin was a nice addition to the Beanie Baby* family in January 1998. Puffins, despite being birds, are more often found swimming in icy waters.

HANG TAG	VALUE 7/1/97	VALUE 1/1/98	VALUE 7/1/98
1ST Generation	–	–	–
2ND Generation	–	–	–
3RD Generation	–	–	–
4TH Generation	–	–	$10
5TH Generation	–	–	$10

*Trademark or name of Ty, Inc., McDonald's Corporation or other distributors of Ty, Inc. dolls, not affiliated with the authors or Schroeder Publishing.

DR. BEANIE

Pugsly is one of the harder to find currents and is a great find on retail shelves. He looks much like the easier to find Wrinkles.

R_X

PUGSLY *

The Pug Dog ▪ #4106
ESTIMATED RETIREMENT: 2001
STATUS: Current
INTRODUCED: 5-11-97 ▪ BIRTHDAY: 5-2-96

HANG TAG	VALUE 7/1/97	VALUE 1/1/98	VALUE 7/1/98
1ST Generation	–	–	–
2ND Generation	–	–	–
3RD Generation	–	–	–
4TH Generation	$10	$10	$10
5TH Generation	–	–	$10

PUNCHERS*

The Lobster ▪ #4026
ESTIMATED PRODUCTION: 750
STATUS: Retired, 1993
INTRODUCED: 1993 ▪ BIRTHDAY: Unknown

The Beanie Babies Collection
Punchers ™ - Style 4026
© 1993 Ty Inc. Oakbrook, IL. USA
All Rights Reserved. Caution:
Remove this tag before giving
toy to a child. For ages 5 and up.
Handmade in Korea.
Surface
Wash.

HANG TAG	VALUE 7/1/97	VALUE 1/1/98	VALUE 7/1/98
1ST Generation	$900	$3,000	$5,500
2ND Generation	–	–	–
3RD Generation	–	–	–
4TH Generation	–	–	–
5TH Generation	–	–	–

Punchers is the rarest Beanie Baby*. He only came with a 1st generation hang tag and very few remain with that tag intact. There are a few ways to tell the difference between Pinchers and Punchers. Punchers has more evenly spaced-out tail segments and has longer feelers. The hang tag reads "Punchers* style 4026." If you have a tagless Beanie Baby* that you are unsure of, check the tush tag. Punchers was made in Korea and Pinchers was made in China.

R

Wingless Quackers is one of the rarest Beanie Babies*. He is especially hard to find with a hang tag that reads "Quacker." Quacker(s) comes with either a first generation or a second generation hang tag. The hang tag came attached on either the neck or on Quacker(s) foot. He was redesigned because he did not easily sit up and also because it made no sense to have a duck with no wings. Add a couple hundred dollars if yours comes with a tag that reads "Quacker."

QUACKERS*

The Duck without Wings ▪ #4024

ESTIMATED PRODUCTION: 2,000

STATUS: Retired, 1-7-95

INTRODUCED: 1994 ▪ BIRTHDAY: Unknown

HANG TAG	VALUE 7/1/97	VALUE 1/1/98	VALUE 7/1/98
1ST Generation	$400	$1,400	$2,600
2ND Generation	$400	$1,400	$2,600
3RD Generation	–	–	–
4TH Generation	–	–	–
5TH Generation	–	–	–

QUACKERS*

The Duck with Wings ▪ #4024

ESTIMATED PRODUCTION: 3,750,000

STATUS: Retired, 5-1-98

INTRODUCED: 1995 ▪ BIRTHDAY: 4-19-94

Quackers is a redesign of wingless Quackers. His wings were a necessary addition since he wouldn't stand up. Quackers has not been a popular Beanie Baby* and will possibly be retired because of that reason.

HANG TAG	VALUE 7/1/97	VALUE 1/1/98	VALUE 7/1/98
1ST Generation	–	–	–
2ND Generation	$200	$500	$1,200
3RD Generation	$30	$45	$125
4TH Generation	$10	$10	$20
5TH Generation	–	–	$20

*Trademark or name of Ty, Inc., McDonald's Corporation or other distributors of Ty, Inc. dolls, not affiliated with the authors or Schroeder Publishing.

 **BEANIE**
DR.

Rx

Radar was introduced in 1996 and was very popular around Halloween. On January 29, 1997, Radar, along with Sparky, was retired for just one day before Ty Inc.* recanted its statement. They were officially retired on May 11, 1997.

RADAR*
The Bat ▪ #4091
ESTIMATED PRODUCTION: 700,000
STATUS: Retired, 5-11-97
INTRODUCED: 1995 ▪ BIRTHDAY: 10-30-95

HANG TAG	VALUE 7/1/97	VALUE 1/1/98	VALUE 7/1/98
1ST Generation	–	–	–
2ND Generation	–	–	–
3RD Generation	$65	$125	$250
4TH Generation	$50	$100	$180
5TH Generation	–	–	–

*Trademark or name of Ty, Inc., McDonald's Corporation or other distributors of Ty, Inc. dolls, not affiliated with the authors or Schroeder Publishing.

RAINBOW *

The Chameleon ▪ #4037

ESTIMATED RETIREMENT: 2000
STATUS: Current
INTRODUCED: 1-1-98 ▪ BIRTHDAY: 10-14-97

HANG TAG	VALUE 7/1/97	VALUE 1/1/98	VALUE 7/1/98
1ST Generation	–	–	–
2ND Generation	–	–	–
3RD Generation	–	–	–
4TH Generation	–	–	$10
5TH Generation	–	–	$10

DR. BEANIE

℞

Rainbow and Iggy entered the Beanie Baby* world and caused confusion. Were the tags switched? Was the material switched? We feel the fabric was mistakenly switched at the factory. We now classify Rainbow as a blue chameleon despite the wording of the poem. See Iggy for more information.

Rx

Rex is the most popular of the Dino trio. He is also the most plentiful. At one time, the only Beanie Babies* that could be found on the retail shelves were the dinosaurs. People would often pass them up. Now, with the Dinosaur trio selling for over $3,000, I'm sure they wish they would have cleaned the shelves of dinosaurs.

REX *

The Tyrannosaurus ▪ #4086

ESTIMATED PRODUCTION: 75,000

STATUS: Retired, 6-15-96

INTRODUCED: 1995 ▪ BIRTHDAY: Unknown

HANG TAG	VALUE 7/1/97	VALUE 1/1/98	VALUE 7/1/98
1ST Generation	–	–	–
2ND Generation	–	–	–
3RD Generation	$250	$475	$1,200
4TH Generation	–	–	–
5TH Generation	–	–	–

*Trademark or name of Ty, Inc., McDonald's Corporation or other distributors of Ty, Inc. dolls, not affiliated with the authors or Schroeder Publishing.

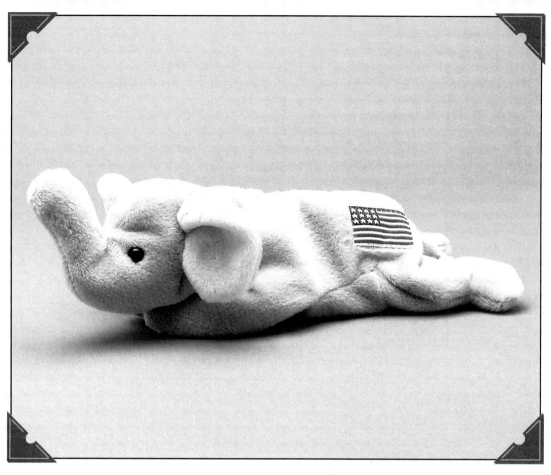

RIGHTY*

The Elephant ▪ #4086

ESTIMATED PRODUCTION: 250,000
STATUS: Retired, 1-1-97
INTRODUCED: 1996 ▪ BIRTHDAY: 7-4-96

HANG TAG	VALUE 7/1/97	VALUE 1/1/98	VALUE 7/1/98
1ST Generation	–	–	–
2ND Generation	–	–	–
3RD Generation	–	–	–
4TH Generation	$60	$150	$300
5TH Generation	–	–	–

*Trademark or name of Ty, Inc., McDonald's Corporation or other distributors of Ty, Inc. dolls, not affiliated with the authors or Schroeder Publishing.

The elephant is the symbol for the Republican Party. Righty is one of four Beanie Babies* decorated with the American flag. The other three are Lefty, Libearty, and Glory. Righty has the same body style as Peanut. Check out the section on Counterfeits on page 266 in this book for a picture of a fake Righty.

Ringo is rumored to have been named after the popular Beatles' drummer. He is relatively easy to find and don't look for him to retire before the next millenium.

RINGO *

The Raccoon ▪ #4014

ESTIMATED RETIREMENT: 2001

STATUS: Current

INTRODUCED: 1996 ▪ BIRTHDAY: 7-14-95

HANG TAG	VALUE 7/1/97	VALUE 1/1/98	VALUE 7/1/98
1ST Generation	–	–	–
2ND Generation	–	–	–
3RD Generation	$30	$45	$100
4TH Generation	$10	$10	$10
5TH Generation	–	–	$10

ROARY *

The Lion ▪ #4069

ESTIMATED RETIREMENT: 2001
STATUS: Current
INTRODUCED: 5-11-97 ▪ BIRTHDAY: 2-20-96

HANG TAG	VALUE 7/1/97	VALUE 1/1/98	VALUE 7/1/98
1ST Generation	–	–	–
2ND Generation	–	–	–
3RD Generation	–	–	–
4TH Generation	$15	$10	$10
5TH Generation	–	–	$10

*Trademark or name of Ty, Inc., McDonald's Corporation or other distributors of Ty, Inc. dolls, not affiliated with the authors or Schroeder Publishing.

Roary the lion is a favorite among many. Look for a lioness friend to join Roary and retire together. Collectors got their first view of Roary on NBC's *Today Show* on March 19, 1997, when Ty, Inc's* vice president was featured on a segment on Beanie Babies*.

℞

 **BEANIE**

℞

Rocket the Blue Jay rocketed into the stores and collectors snatched him up. Collectors wondered why two of the birds chosen to be Beanie Babies* are considered to be pests, Caw the Crow and now Rocket. Don't get us wrong, we think Rocket is a winner.

ROCKET*

The Blue Jay ▪ #4202

ESTIMATED RETIREMENT: 2002

STATUS: Current

INTRODUCED: 5-30-98 ▪ BIRTHDAY: 3-12-97

HANG TAG	VALUE 7/1/97	VALUE 1/1/98	VALUE 7/1/98
1ST Generation	–	–	–
2ND Generation	–	–	–
3RD Generation	–	–	–
4TH Generation	–	–	–
5TH Generation	–	–	$20

ROVER*

The Red Dog ▪ #4101

ESTIMATED PRODUCTION: 3,500,000

STATUS: Retired, 5-1-98

INTRODUCED: 1996 ▪ BIRTHDAY: 5-30-96

HANG TAG	VALUE 7/1/97	VALUE 1/1/98	VALUE 7/1/98
1ST Generation	–	–	–
2ND Generation	–	–	–
3RD Generation	–	–	–
4TH Generation	$10	$10	$25
5TH Generation	–	–	$25

*Trademark or name of Ty, Inc., McDonald's Corporation or other distributors of Ty, Inc. dolls, not affiliated with the authors or Schroeder Publishing.

℞

Rover was part of a Fannie May* promotion for Christmas 1997. He was included with a box of Fannie May* chocolates. See the Promotion Section on page 247 of this book for details.

 DR. BEANIE

R_x

Scoop is one of the harder to find current Beanie Babies*. Expect him to retire next year. He shares his fabric with Crunch the shark. Scoop is a favorite with many collectors because he shares his birthday with the late Princess Diana.

SCOOP*

The Pelican ▪ #4107

ESTIMATED RETIREMENT: 1999
STATUS: Current
INTRODUCED: 1996 ▪ BIRTHDAY: 7-1-96

HANG TAG	VALUE 7/1/97	VALUE 1/1/98	VALUE 7/1/98
1ST Generation	–	–	–
2ND Generation	–	–	–
3RD Generation	–	–	–
4TH Generation	$10	$10	$10
5TH Generation	–	–	$10

SCOTTIE *

The Scottish Terrier ▪ #4102

ESTIMATED PRODUCTION: 3,000,000

STATUS: Retired, 5-1-98

INTRODUCED: 1996 ▪ BIRTHDAY: 6-15-96

HANG TAG	VALUE 7/1/97	VALUE 1/1/98	VALUE 7/1/98
1ST Generation	–	–	–
2ND Generation	–	–	–
3RD Generation	–	–	–
4TH Generation	$10	$10	$30
5TH Generation	–	–	$30

*Trademark or name of Ty, Inc., McDonald's Corporation or other distributors of Ty, Inc. dolls, not affiliated with the authors or Schroeder Publishing.

Scottie is one of the five napped Beanie Babies*, along with Curly, Fleece, Gigi, and Tuffy. Scotties can be found with two different birthdays on their hang tags. The correct birthday is 6-15-96. The incorrect birthday is 6-3-96. Both versions have equal value, but make an interesting addition to your collection.

Seamore the Seal almost tripled in value in two short months. Be sure to keep Seamore in a dust free environment to protect this Beanie Baby*. Seamore was chosen to be part of the 1997 McDonald's* Teenie Beanie* set.

R

SEAMORE*

The Seal ▪ #4029

ESTIMATED PRODUCTION: 750,000
STATUS: Retired, 10-1-97
INTRODUCED: 1994 ▪ BIRTHDAY: 12-14-96

HANG TAG	VALUE 7/1/97	VALUE 1/1/98	VALUE 7/1/98
1ST Generation	$55	$175	$525
2ND Generation	$35	$150	$375
3RD Generation	$25	$105	$240
4TH Generation	$10	$75	$180
5TH Generation	–	–	–

SEAWEED*

The Otter ▪ #4080

ESTIMATED RETIREMENT: 1999
STATUS: Current

INTRODUCED: 1996 ▪ BIRTHDAY: 3-19-96

HANG TAG	VALUE 7/1/97	VALUE 1/1/98	VALUE 7/1/98
1ST Generation	–	–	–
2ND Generation	–	–	–
3RD Generation	$30	$45	$95
4TH Generation	$10	$10	$10
5TH Generation	–	–	$10

Rx

Most Beanie Babies* can be washed in cool water in the washing machine with the hang tags removed. The exceptions are Beanie Babies* with felt pieces such as Seaweed. It is best to use a dry brush to remove dirt and lint. See the Storage and Care of Beanie Babies* Section on page 7 in the book for more information.

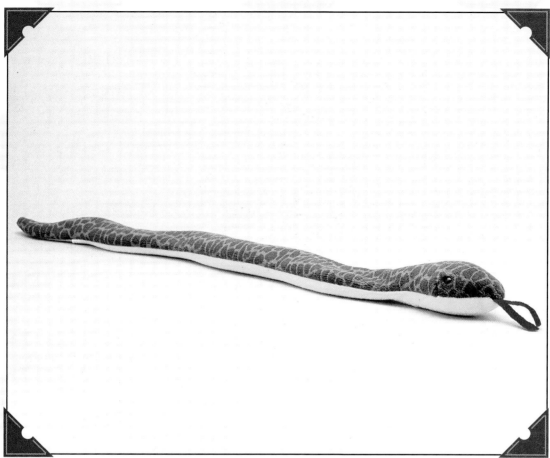

 **BEANIE**
DR.

Rx

Slither was produced in mid-1994. He goes against the hand-held size of all other Beanie Babies*. He measures 23 inches long! He is truly a great Beanie Baby* to own and a favorite of many collectors. His fabric is identical to that of Ally and Speedy. His tongue was not secured firmly so many played-with Slithers are tongueless which decreases his value by 75%.

SLITHER*

The Snake ▪ #4031

ESTIMATED PRODUCTION: 20,000
STATUS: Retired 6-15-95
INTRODUCED: 1994 ▪ BIRTHDAY: Unknown

HANG TAG	VALUE 7/1/97	VALUE 1/1/98	VALUE 7/1/98
1ST Generation	$650	$1,100	$2,800
2ND Generation	$600	$1,100	$2,800
3RD Generation	$600	$1,000	$2,800
4TH Generation	–	–	–
5TH Generation	–	–	–

*Trademark or name of Ty, Inc., McDonald's Corporation or other distributors of Ty, Inc. dolls, not affiliated with the authors or Schroeder Publishing.

SLY *

The Brown Bellied Fox ▪ #4115

ESTIMATED PRODUCTION: 150,000

STATUS: Retired, 8-6-96

INTRODUCED: 1996 ▪ BIRTHDAY: 9-12-96

Brown bellied Sly was the first version of Sly. He was introduced in mid-1996. He was redesigned in late 1996 because he didn't look like a real fox. The only change made was the color of his belly. This new version looked much more like a real fox.

HANG TAG	VALUE 7/1/97	VALUE 1/1/98	VALUE 7/1/98
1ST Generation	–	–	–
2ND Generation	–	–	–
3RD Generation	–	–	–
4TH Generation	$60	$145	$200
5TH Generation	–	–	–

*Trademark or name of Ty, Inc., McDonald's Corporation or other distributors of Ty, Inc. dolls, not affiliated with the authors or Schroeder Publishing.

 **BEANIE** **R̃**

Sly is the only fox in the Beanie Baby* family. Sly was originally produced with a brown belly, but was changed soon after. The new Sly is a more accurate representation of what a fox really looks like. Sly was one of many Beanie Babies* used in the Mega Fun Packs. See Special Interest Section on page 238 of this book for more details.

SLY*

The White Bellied Fox ▪ #4115

ESTIMATED RETIREMENT: 2000
STATUS: Current
INTRODUCED: 1996 ▪ BIRTHDAY: 9-12-96

HANG TAG	VALUE 7/1/97	VALUE 1/1/98	VALUE 7/1/98
1ST Generation	–	–	–
2ND Generation	–	–	–
3RD Generation	–	–	–
4TH Generation	$10	$10	$10
5TH Generation	–	–	–

SMOOCHY *

The Frog ▪ #4039

ESTIMATED RETIREMENT: 2003

STATUS: Current

INTRODUCED: 1-1-98 ▪ BIRTHDAY: 10-1-97

HANG TAG	VALUE 7/1/97	VALUE 1/1/98	VALUE 7/1/98
1ST Generation	–	–	–
2ND Generation	–	–	–
3RD Generation	–	–	–
4TH Generation	–	–	$10
5TH Generation	–	–	$10

 **DR. BEANIE** ℞

Smoochy is the second frog in the Beanie Baby* family. He was released on January 1, 1998, replacing Legs, which retired three months before Smoochy's introduction. Already, Smoochy has proved to be much more popular than Legs. A prototype of Smoochy was made having red feet but Ty changed its mind and went with the Smoochy that we have today.

Rx

There are five cats in the "ip" family: Snip, Zip, Chip, Nip, and Flip. Only Snip and Chip are still current. Many people were expecting another "ip" cat when new Beanie Babies* were introduced in January, but Ty Inc.* introduced Prance and Pounce, breaking the trend.

SNIP*

The Siamese Cat ▪ #4120

ESTIMATED RETIREMENT: 2000
STATUS: Current
INTRODUCED: 1-1-97 ▪ BIRTHDAY: 10-22-96

HANG TAG	VALUE 7/1/97	VALUE 1/1/98	VALUE 7/1/98
1ST Generation	–	–	–
2ND Generation	–	–	–
3RD Generation	–	–	–
4TH Generation	$10	$10	$10
5TH Generation	–	–	$10

*Trademark or name of Ty, Inc., McDonald's Corporation or other distributors of Ty, Inc. dolls, not affiliated with the authors or Schroeder Publishing.

143

SNORT *

The Bull ▪ #4002

ESTIMATED RETIREMENT: 2002

STATUS: Current

INTRODUCED: 1-1-97 ▪ BIRTHDAY: 5-15-95

HANG TAG	VALUE 7/1/97	VALUE 1/1/98	VALUE 7/1/98
1ST Generation	–	–	–
2ND Generation	–	–	–
3RD Generation	–	–	–
4TH Generation	$10	$10	$10
5TH Generation	–	–	$10

DR. BEANIE

R

Snort shares the same birthday as the retired Tabasco. Snort's and Tabasco's poems are identical except for their names. Some Canadian Snorts produced in 1997 have Tabasco poems. This mistake adds about $20 to the value of the Beanie Baby*. Snort was the replacement for Tabasco and looks identical to him, except for his cream paws. Snort was one of the three worst sellers in 1997 along with Gracie and Crunch.

Rx

Snowball was one of the five holiday introductions of late 1997. He was the second non-animal to be produced. Spooky is the other one. After a very short life, Snowball was retired on January 1, 1998. This limited production of Snowball makes him an ideal Beanie Baby* to quickly appreciate in value.

SNOWBALL*

The Snowman ▪ #4201

ESTIMATED PRODUCTION: 200,000

STATUS: Retired, 1-1-98

INTRODUCED: 10-1-97 ▪ BIRTHDAY: 12-22-96

HANG TAG	VALUE 7/1/97	VALUE 1/1/98	VALUE 7/1/98
1ST Generation	–	–	–
2ND Generation	–	–	–
3RD Generation	–	–	–
4TH Generation	–	$25	$45
5TH Generation	–	–	–

*Trademark or name of Ty, Inc., McDonald's Corporation or other distributors of Ty, Inc. dolls, not affiliated with the authors or Schroeder Publishing.

SPARKY*

The Dalmatian ▪ #4100

ESTIMATED PRODUCTION: 750,000
STATUS: Retired, 5-11-97
INTRODUCED: 1996 ▪ BIRTHDAY: 2-27-96

Rx

On January 29, 1997, Ty Inc.* announced that Sparky was retired. On January 30, the next day, Ty Inc.* said that it was a mistake and he was not retired. Ty Inc.* officially retired Sparky on Mother's Day of that year. The last Sparkys to be produced had Dotty tags. This ruined the announcement of a new Dalmatian named Dotty. Sparky was retired because the name "Sparky" is a registered trademark of the National Fire Protection Association (N.F.P.A.).

HANG TAG	VALUE 7/1/97	VALUE 1/1/98	VALUE 7/1/98
1ST Generation	–	–	–
2ND Generation	–	–	–
3RD Generation	–	–	–
4TH Generation	$35	$65	$175
5TH Generation	–	–	–

Rx

Speedy was retired on October 1, 1997. Even though he was retired, he was easy to find on all retail shelves. Because of this, it took a while for Speedy's price to go up. Speedy's price is slowly escalating now. Make sure you get a hold of Speedy while he is cheap because he will continue to appreciate in value. The material on Speedy's back is the same that can be found on Ally the Alligator and Slither the Snake.

SPEEDY*

The Turtle ▪ #4030

ESTIMATED PRODUCTION: 2,500,000

STATUS: Retired, 10-1-97

INTRODUCED: 1994 ▪ BIRTHDAY: 8-14-94

HANG TAG	VALUE 7/1/97	VALUE 1/1/98	VALUE 7/1/98
1ST Generation	$50	$120	$400
2ND Generation	$35	$100	$250
3RD Generation	$25	$50	$125
4TH Generation	$10	$15	$35
5TH Generation	–	–	–

SPIKE *

The Rhinoceros ▪ #4060

ESTIMATED RETIREMENT: 2000
STATUS: Current
INTRODUCED: 1996 ▪ BIRTHDAY: 8-13-96

HANG TAG	VALUE 7/1/97	VALUE 1/1/98	VALUE 7/1/98
1ST Generation	–	–	–
2ND Generation	–	–	–
3RD Generation	–	–	–
4TH Generation	$10	$10	$10
5TH Generation	–	–	$10

Spike is favorite among many boys. In fall of 1997, Spike became very hard to find but is now more plentiful. Many collectors thought he would be a 1997 retiree due to his scarcity. Obviously, they were wrong.

Spinner was difficult to find when first released. Soon he was plentiful and often is the last Beanie Baby* left on the store shelves. Spinner's back is made with the same material that was on the old Stripes. Expect Spinner to be around until at least next Halloween. Spinners began arriving with "Creepy" tush tags in April 1998. We still are left wondering who is Creepy? Rumor has it that he will be a snail.

SPINNER*

The Spider ▪ #4036

ESTIMATED RETIREMENT: 1999
STATUS: CURRENT

INTRODUCED: 10-1-97 ▪ BIRTHDAY: 10-28-96

HANG TAG	VALUE 7/1/97	VALUE 1/1/98	VALUE 7/1/98
1ST Generation	–	–	–
2ND Generation	–	–	–
3RD Generation	–	–	–
4TH Generation	–	$20	$10
5TH Generation	–	–	$10

SPLASH*

The Whale ▪ #4022

ESTIMATED PRODUCTION: 1,000,000

STATUS: Retired, 5-11-97

INTRODUCED: 1994 ▪ BIRTHDAY: 7-8-93

R

Splash was retired on Mother's Day in 1997. She could be found for around $50 all the way up to November of 1997. Then, all of a sudden, her price started going up rapidly. Splash was one of the original nine.

HANG TAG	VALUE 7/1/97	VALUE 1/1/98	VALUE 7/1/98
1ST Generation	$110	$170	$450
2ND Generation	$75	$140	$350
3RD Generation	$50	$90	$225
4TH Generation	$35	$60	$140
5TH Generation	–	–	–

*Trademark or name of Ty, Inc., McDonald's Corporation or other distributors of Ty, Inc. dolls, not affiliated with the authors or Schroeder Publishing.

Spook is the only Beanie Baby* with the designer's name on the hang tag. The tag reads "Designed by Jenna Boldebuck." Jenna is the teenage daughter of Ty Warner's friend. Spook has a 3rd generation hang tag and a "V" shaped mouth. Spook's name was changed to Spooky prior to the 1996 Beanie Baby* introductions. Spook is very hard to find and we are surprised he is not a $1,000 Beanie Baby*!

R̽

SPOOK*

The Ghost ▪ #4090

ESTIMATED PRODUCTION: 5000

STATUS: Retired, 1995

INTRODUCED: 1995 ▪ BIRTHDAY: Unknown

HANG TAG	VALUE 7/1/97	VALUE 1/1/98	VALUE 7/1/98
1ST Generation	–	–	–
2ND Generation	–	–	–
3RD Generation	$150	$250	$900
4TH Generation	–	–	–
5TH Generation	–	–	–

SPOOKY *

The Ghost ▪ #4090

ESTIMATED PRODUCTION: 2,000,000

STATUS: Retired, 1-1-98

INTRODUCED: 1996 ▪ BIRTHDAY: 10-31-95

HANG TAG	VALUE 7/1/97	VALUE 1/1/98	VALUE 7/1/98
1ST Generation	–	–	–
2ND Generation	–	–	–
3RD Generation	$40	$50	$120
4TH Generation	$20	$25	$40
5TH Generation	–	–	–

*Trademark or name of Ty, Inc., McDonald's Corporation or other distributors of Ty, Inc. dolls, not affiliated with the authors or Schroeder Publishing.

Spooky was introduced in 1996. He is generally found with a 4th generation tag, but there are some 3rd generation tags in existence. Spooky was never plentiful while a current. He hasn't gone up much since his retirement, but just wait, he will eventually. Spook (Spooky) was the first non-animal Beanie Baby*.

Spotless Spot was one of the original nine Beanie Babies*. He can be found with either a 1st or 2nd generation hang tag. Not many perfect condition Spots can be found because of his white material. Most appear more of an off-white color. Keep Spot away from anything that could make him dirty and keep him in a container that will not allow dust to settle on him.

R̰

SPOT*

The Dog Without a Spot ▪ #4000

ESTIMATED PRODUCTION: 2,000
STATUS: Retired, 4-13-94
INTRODUCED: 1994 ▪ BIRTHDAY: Unknown

HANG TAG	VALUE 7/1/97	VALUE 1/1/98	VALUE 7/1/98
1ST Generation	$600	$1,800	$2,500
2ND Generation	$575	$1,400	$2,400
3RD Generation	–	–	–
4TH Generation	–	–	–
5TH Generation	–	–	–

*Trademark or name of Ty, Inc., McDonald's Corporation or other distributors of Ty, Inc. dolls, not affiliated with the authors or Schroeder Publishing.

RETIRED

SPOT *

The Dog with a Spot ▪ #4000

ESTIMATED PRODUCTION: 1,750,000
STATUS: Retired, 10-1-97
INTRODUCED: 1994 ▪ BIRTHDAY: 1-3-93

HANG TAG	VALUE 7/1/97	VALUE 1/1/98	VALUE 7/1/98
1ST Generation	–	–	–
2ND Generation	$200	$450	$1,100
3RD Generation	$30	$60	$150
4TH Generation	$10	$35	$65
5TH Generation	–	–	–

*Trademark or name of Ty, Inc., McDonald's Corporation or other distributors of Ty, Inc. dolls, not affiliated with the authors or Schroeder Publishing.

Rx

Spot is a redesign of the old spotless Spot. It made no sense for a dog named Spot to not have a spot, so Ty Inc.* changed that. Spot has been a great seller since his retirement. Second generation Spots are in high demand as their tags can be switched to a Spot without a Spot.

 **R**x

Spunky is so adorable he is sure to be a favorite of all Beanie Baby* collectors. The main reason for his popularity is his realistic looking appearance. He is a must for all cocker spaniel owners. Spunky is the first Beanie Baby* to have "long-haired" fuzzy ears.

SPUNKY*

The Cocker Spaniel ▪ #4184
ESTIMATED RETIREMENT: 2003
STATUS: Current
INTRODUCED: 1-1-98 ▪ BIRTHDAY: 1-14-97

HANG TAG	VALUE 7/1/97	VALUE 1/1/98	VALUE 7/1/98
1ST Generation	–	–	–
2ND Generation	–	–	–
3RD Generation	–	–	–
4TH Generation	–	–	–
5TH Generation	–	–	$10

SQUEALER*

The Pig ▪ #4005

ESTIMATED PRODUCTION: 3,250,000
STATUS: Retired, 5-1-98
INTRODUCED: 1994 ▪ BIRTHDAY: 4-23-93

Squealer was one of the original nine Beanie Babies*. He is highly sought after with his original 1st generation hang tag. We expect this 1st generation tagged Squealer will skyrocket in value, especially now that he has retired.

HANG TAG	VALUE 7/1/97	VALUE 1/1/98	VALUE 7/1/98
1ST Generation	$60	$140	$450
2ND Generation	$40	$120	$275
3RD Generation	$25	$50	$125
4TH Generation	$10	$10	$30
5TH Generation	–	–	$35

 **Rx**

Steg is a brownish-green tie-dyed stegosaurus. He usually can be found with mainly rust and brown coloring. Steg, like other dinosaurs, is hard to find and very sought after.

STEG*

The Stegosaurus ▪ #4087

ESTIMATED PRODUCTION: 60,000
STATUS: Retired, 6-15-96
INTRODUCED: 1995 ▪ BIRTHDAY: Unknown

HANG TAG	VALUE 7/1/97	VALUE 1/1/98	VALUE 7/1/98
1ST Generation	–	–	–
2ND Generation	–	–	–
3RD Generation	$300	$475	$1,200
4TH Generation	–	–	–
5TH Generation	–	–	–

*Trademark or name of Ty, Inc., McDonald's Corporation or other distributors of Ty, Inc. dolls, not affiliated with the authors or Schroeder Publishing.

STING *

The Stingray ▪ #4077

ESTIMATED PRODUCTION: 300,000

STATUS: Retired, 1-1-97

INTRODUCED: 1995 ▪ BIRTHDAY: 8-27-95

HANG TAG	VALUE 7/1/97	VALUE 1/1/98	VALUE 7/1/98
1ST Generation	–	–	–
2ND Generation	–	–	–
3RD Generation	$80	$200	$425
4TH Generation	$60	$120	$240
5TH Generation	–	–	–

Sting is the most expensive January 1997 retiree after the American trio. He is one of the bestsellers in the Beanie Baby* family. He shares his material with Bronty, Hissy, and Rainbow. Hopefully, Ty Inc.* will introduce some more marine Beanie Babies* into the Beanie Baby* family.

R_x

Stinger the Scorpion has been a favorite with young boys. He has not been a popular Beanie Baby* with most collectors. History has shown that many Beanie Babies* that began their life with slow sales end up being in high demand at a later date.

STINGER *

The Scorpion ▪ #4193

ESTIMATED RETIREMENT: 2002

STATUS: Current

INTRODUCED: 5-30-98 ▪ BIRTHDAY: 9-29-97

HANG TAG	VALUE 7/1/97	VALUE 1/1/98	VALUE 7/1/98
1ST Generation	–	–	–
2ND Generation	–	–	–
3RD Generation	–	–	–
4TH Generation	–	–	–
5TH Generation	–	–	$15

STINKY[*]

The Skunk ▪ #4017

ESTIMATED RETIREMENT: 1999
STATUS: Current
INTRODUCED: 1995 ▪ BIRTHDAY: 2-13-95

HANG TAG	VALUE 7/1/97	VALUE 1/1/98	VALUE 7/1/98
1ST Generation	–	–	–
2ND Generation	–	–	–
3RD Generation	$25	$45	$95
4TH Generation	$10	$10	$10
5TH Generation	–	–	–

R

Stinky has not been a popular Beanie Baby*, so look for an early retirement. He should be around until sometime next year. Stinkys have been found with several incorrect tush tags. This does not increase the value.

R̲x

Stretch was introduced in January 1998, with nine other Beanie Babies*. Stretch was scarce at first and commanded top dollars. Her price began dropping as she became more available. Stretch has the same basic design as Pinky. She is the first Beanie Baby* to have raised fuzz.

STRETCH *

The Ostrich ▪ #4082

ESTIMATED RETIREMENT: 2000
STATUS: Current
INTRODUCED: 1-1-98 ▪ BIRTHDAY: 9-21-97

HANG TAG	VALUE 7/1/97	VALUE 1/1/98	VALUE 7/1/98
1ST Generation	–	–	–
2ND Generation	–	–	–
3RD Generation	–	–	–
4TH Generation	–	–	$10
5TH Generation	–	–	$10

STRIPES *

The Gold and Black Tiger ▪ #4065

ESTIMATED PRODUCTION: 75,000
STATUS: Retired, 6-3-96
INTRODUCED: 1995 ▪ BIRTHDAY: Unknown

HANG TAG	VALUE 7/1/97	VALUE 1/1/98	VALUE 7/1/98
1ST Generation	–	–	–
2ND Generation	–	–	–
3RD Generation	$150	$250	$500
4TH Generation	–	–	–
5TH Generation	–	–	–

Gold and black Stripes was introduced in mid-1995. He was redesigned in mid to late 1996. He was probably changed because he was quite ugly and did not resemble a real tiger. The new Stripes was produced about six months after dark Stripes was retired. A fuzzy belly version was also produced, see next page.

 **Dr. BEANIE**

Rx

Fuzzy belly Stripes is extremely rare. He is actually an oddity, but since he was produced like this for a short period of time, many consider him an actual Beanie Baby*. Just remember, royal blue Peanut was a mistake too.

STRIPES*

The Gold and Black Tiger with Fuzzy Belly ▪ #4065

ESTIMATED PRODUCTION: 5,000

STATUS: Retired, 1996

INTRODUCED: 1996 ▪ BIRTHDAY: Unknown

HANG TAG	VALUE 7/1/97	VALUE 1/1/98	VALUE 7/1/98
1ST Generation	–	–	–
2ND Generation	–	–	–
3RD Generation	$300	$600	$1,400
4TH Generation	–	–	–
5TH Generation	–	–	–

STRIPES*

The Caramel and Black Tiger ▪ #4065

ESTIMATED PRODUCTION: 3,500,000

STATUS: Retired, 5-1-98

INTRODUCED: 1996 ▪ BIRTHDAY: 6-11-95

HANG TAG	VALUE 7/1/97	VALUE 1/1/98	VALUE 7/1/98
1ST Generation	–	–	–
2ND Generation	–	–	–
3RD Generation	–	–	–
4TH Generation	$10	$10	$25
5TH Generation	–	–	$25

*Trademark or name of Ty, Inc., McDonald's Corporation or other distributors of Ty, Inc. dolls, not affiliated with the authors or Schroeder Publishing.

DR. BEANIE

Rx

Stripes was originally made with a dark gold material and more stripes. He was changed to his current form in late 1996. The current Stripes is only produced with a 4th and 5th generation hang tags. Stripes was used for the Chinese Year of the Tiger promotion. See the Promotion Section on page 246 of this book for details and photo. The Detroit Tigers also used Stripes for a promotion, see page 233. A fuzzy belly version has been found, as shown on page 261.

Rx

Strut was an immediate response to the retiring of the name Doodle. Strut is the exact same Beanie Baby* as Doodle, except for their names on their tags. Everything else is identical, including their style numbers. Do not wash Strut or Doodle due to the felt on the Beanie Baby*. See Storage and Care of Your Beanie Babies* Section on page 7 of this book for more details.

STRUT *

The Rooster ▪ #4171

ESTIMATED RETIREMENT: 2001
STATUS: Current
INTRODUCED: 1997 ▪ BIRTHDAY: 3-8-96

HANG TAG	VALUE 7/1/97	VALUE 1/1/98	VALUE 7/1/98
1ST Generation	–	–	–
2ND Generation	–	–	–
3RD Generation	–	–	–
4TH Generation	–	$10	$10
5TH Generation	–	–	$10

TABASCO *

The Bull ▪ #4002

ESTIMATED PRODUCTION: 350,000

STATUS: Retired, 1-1-97

INTRODUCED: 1995 ▪ BIRTHDAY: 5-15-95

HANG TAG	VALUE 7/1/97	VALUE 1/1/98	VALUE 7/1/98
1ST Generation	–	–	–
2ND Generation	–	–	–
3RD Generation	$190	$220	$325
4TH Generation	$150	$175	$225
5TH Generation	–	–	–

R

Tabasco was a big hit when he was a current Beanie Baby*. His poem alludes to the fact that he likes the Chicago Bulls. Basketball fans as well as Beanie Baby* collectors started buying up all the Tabascos. Rumor has it that Tabasco was retired due to a conflict with the Tabasco Sauce Company.

*Trademark or name of Ty, Inc., McDonald's Corporation or other distributors of Ty, Inc. dolls, not affiliated with the authors or Schroeder Publishing.

Rx

Seven line Tank was the first version of Tank produced. He is usually found with a 3rd generation hang tag, but a few can be found with 4th generation tags.

TANK *

The Armadillo with Seven Lines (no shell) ▪ #4031

ESTIMATED PRODUCTION: 75,000

STATUS: Retired, 1996

INTRODUCED: 1995 ▪ BIRTHDAY: Unknown

HANG TAG	VALUE 7/1/97	VALUE 1/1/98	VALUE 7/1/98
1ST Generation	–	–	–
2ND Generation	–	–	–
3RD Generation	$65	$150	$275
4TH Generation	$50	$100	$175
5TH Generation	–	–	–

*Trademark or name of Ty, Inc., McDonald's Corporation or other distributors of Ty, Inc. dolls, not affiliated with the authors or Schroeder Publishing.

167

TANK*

The Armadillo with Nine Lines (no shell) ▪ #4031

ESTIMATED PRODUCTION: 125,000

STATUS: Retired, 1996

INTRODUCED: 1996 ▪ BIRTHDAY: 2-22-95

Nine line Tank is the second version of Tank produced. He has a slightly more rounded nose than the seven line Tank. They are both the same length. Nine line Tank was made when 4th generation tags first came out. He was soon changed to the Tank with a shell.

HANG TAG	VALUE 7/1/97	VALUE 1/1/98	VALUE 7/1/98
1ST Generation	–	–	–
2ND Generation	–	–	–
3RD Generation	–	–	–
4TH Generation	$50	$150	$200
5TH Generation	–	–	–

*Trademark or name of Ty, Inc., McDonald's Corporation or other distributors of Ty, Inc. dolls, not affiliated with the authors or Schroeder Publishing.

 **Rx**

Tank was retired on October 1, 1997, after several style changes. He continues to escalate in value, especially since many collectors missed purchasing him while he was a current.

TANK*

The Armadillo with Shell ▪ #4031

ESTIMATED PRODUCTION: 1,000,000
STATUS: Retired, 10-1-97
INTRODUCED: 1996 ▪ BIRTHDAY: 2-22-95

HANG TAG	VALUE 7/1/97	VALUE 1/1/98	VALUE 7/1/98
1ST Generation	–	–	–
2ND Generation	–	–	–
3RD Generation	–	–	–
4TH Generation	$10	$50	$80
5TH Generation	–	–	–

*Trademark or name of Ty, Inc., McDonald's Corporation or other distributors of Ty, Inc. dolls, not affiliated with the authors or Schroeder Publishing.

169

TEDDY *

Old Face Brown ▪ #4050

ESTIMATED PRODUCTION: 5,000
STATUS: Retired, 1-7-95
INTRODUCED: 1994 ▪ BIRTHDAY: Unknown

HANG TAG	VALUE 7/1/97	VALUE 1/1/98	VALUE 7/1/98
1ST Generation	$500	$1,850	$4,200
2ND Generation	$500	$1,800	$4,100
3RD Generation	–	–	–
4TH Generation	–	–	–
5TH Generation	–	–	–

The old face brown Teddy is by far the rarest of all the Teddies. He sells for almost twice as much as the other old face bears and is a great Beanie Baby* to get your hands on. Make sure that it isn't a new face brown with the string cut above his nose to make it appear old face. The eyes on an old face Teddy are on the outside of the "V" shaped seam on their face.

*Trademark or name of Ty, Inc., McDonald's Corporation or other distributors of Ty, Inc. dolls, not affiliated with the authors or Schroeder Publishing.

RETIRED

 **BEANIE**
DR.

R_x

New face brown Teddy is the only colored Teddy that is relatively common. No other colored Teddy was produced with a 4th generation hang tag. No one knows why Ty Inc.* decided to keep the new face brown around while they retired all the other Teddys. Expect brown new face Teddy to escalate in value now that he too is retired.

TEDDY*

New Face Brown ▪ #4050

ESTIMATED PRODUCTION: 750,000
STATUS: Retired, 10-1-97
INTRODUCED: 1-7-95 ▪ BIRTHDAY: 11-28-95

HANG TAG	VALUE 7/1/97	VALUE 1/1/98	VALUE 7/1/98
1ST Generation	–	–	–
2ND Generation	$85	$500	$1,000
3RD Generation	$20	$100	$250
4TH Generation	$10	$50	$100
5TH Generation	–	–	–

*Trademark or name of Ty, Inc., McDonald's Corporation or other distributors of Ty, Inc. dolls, not affiliated with the authors or Schroeder Publishing.

171

TEDDY*

Old Face Cranberry ▪ #4052

ESTIMATED PRODUCTION: 10,000
STATUS: Retired, 1-7-95
INTRODUCED: 1994 ▪ BIRTHDAY: Unknown

Rx

The old face Teddies have eyes that are set on the outside of the "V" shaped seam on its face. They can be found with both 1st and 2nd generation hang tags.

HANG TAG	VALUE 7/1/97	VALUE 1/1/98	VALUE 7/1/98
1ST Generation	$400	$1,100	$2,400
2ND Generation	$300	$1,100	$2,300
3RD Generation	–	–	–
4TH Generation	–	–	–
5TH Generation	–	–	–

*Trademark or name of Ty, Inc., McDonald's Corporation or other distributors of Ty, Inc. dolls, not affiliated with the authors or Schroeder Publishing.

 **BEANIE**
DR.

R

Many people believe that new face Teddies are rarer than old face Teddies. This is not true. The Teddies, with the exception of the brown ones, were all made for the same period of time. The new faced bears seem to be more popular though. The new face cranberry and new face violet Teddies both come with green ribbons tied around their neck.

TEDDY*

New Face Cranberry ▪ #4052

ESTIMATED PRODUCTION: 15,000
STATUS: Retired, 1-7-96
INTRODUCED: 1995 ▪ BIRTHDAY: Unknown

HANG TAG	VALUE 7/1/97	VALUE 1/1/98	VALUE 7/1/98
1ST Generation	–	–	–
2ND Generation	$500	$1,200	$2,450
3RD Generation	$400	$1,200	$2,350
4TH Generation	–	–	–
5TH Generation	–	–	–

*Trademark or name of Ty, Inc., McDonald's Corporation or other distributors of Ty, Inc. dolls, not affiliated with the authors or Schroeder Publishing.

TEDDY*

Old Face Jade ▪ #4057

ESTIMATED PRODUCTION: 15,000
STATUS: Retired, 1-7-95
INTRODUCED: 1994 ▪ BIRTHDAY: Unknown

 **DR. BEANIE**

Rx

There are an even dozen colored bears in the Beanie Baby* family. If you can't afford these older bears, get a hold of some of the newer, less expensive bears such as Curly, Valentino, or Fortune.

HANG TAG	VALUE 7/1/97	VALUE 1/1/98	VALUE 7/1/98
1ST Generation	$400	$1,100	$2,400
2ND Generation	$300	$1,100	$2,300
3RD Generation	–	–	–
4TH Generation	–	–	–
5TH Generation	–	–	–

*Trademark or name of Ty, Inc., McDonald's Corporation or other distributors of Ty, Inc. dolls, not affiliated with the authors or Schroeder Publishing.

 **DR. BEANIE**

Rx

The new face Teddies come with 2nd or 3rd generation hang tags and a 1993 black and white tush tag. The new face jade comes with a cranberry ribbon tied around his neck.

TEDDY*

New Face Jade ▪ #4057

ESTIMATED PRODUCTION: 15,000

STATUS: Retired, 1-7-96

INTRODUCED: 1995 ▪ BIRTHDAY: Unknown

HANG TAG	VALUE 7/1/97	VALUE 1/1/98	VALUE 7/1/98
1ST Generation	–	–	–
2ND Generation	$500	$1,200	$2,450
3RD Generation	$400	$1,200	$2,350
4TH Generation	–	–	–
5TH Generation	–	–	–

TEDDY *

Old Face Magenta ▪ #4056

ESTIMATED PRODUCTION: 15,000

STATUS: Retired, 1-7-95

INTRODUCED: 1994 ▪ BIRTHDAY: Unknown

DR. BEANIE

℞

The old face Teddies were made in both China and Korea and there can be slight differences in color because of this.

HANG TAG	VALUE 7/1/97	VALUE 1/1/98	VALUE 7/1/98
1ST Generation	$400	$1,100	$2,400
2ND Generation	$300	$1,100	$2,300
3RD Generation	–	–	–
4TH Generation	–	–	–
5TH Generation	–	–	–

*Trademark or name of Ty, Inc., McDonald's Corporation or other distributors of Ty, Inc. dolls, not affiliated with the authors or Schroeder Publishing.

Only the new face Teddies came with ribbons around their necks. The new face magenta comes with a pink ribbon tied around his neck.

R

TEDDY*

New Face Magenta ▪ #4056

ESTIMATED PRODUCTION: 15,000

STATUS: Retired, 1-7-96

INTRODUCED: 1995 ▪ BIRTHDAY: Unknown

HANG TAG	VALUE 7/1/97	VALUE 1/1/98	VALUE 7/1/98
1ST Generation	–	–	–
2ND Generation	$500	$1,200	$2,450
3RD Generation	$400	$1,200	$2,350
4TH Generation	–	–	–
5TH Generation	–	–	–

*Trademark or name of Ty, Inc., McDonald's Corporation or other distributors of Ty, Inc. dolls, not affiliated with the authors or Schroeder Publishing.

TEDDY *

Old Face Teal ▪ #4051

ESTIMATED PRODUCTION: 15,000

STATUS: Retired, 1-7-95

INTRODUCED: 1994 ▪ BIRTHDAY: Unknown

℞

The teal colored Teddies are often confused with the jade colored Teddies. The teal Teddy is a lighter, brighter green-blue color.

HANG TAG	VALUE 7/1/97	VALUE 1/1/98	VALUE 7/1/98
1ST Generation	$400	$1,100	$2,400
2ND Generation	$300	$1,100	$2,300
3RD Generation	–	–	–
4TH Generation	–	–	–
5TH Generation	–	–	–

*Trademark or name of Ty, Inc., McDonald's Corporation or other distributors of Ty, Inc. dolls, not affiliated with the authors or Schroeder Publishing.

R

The new face Teddies sometimes came with 3rd generation hang tags. On these hang tags, the style number of the colored Teddy is listed.

TEDDY*

New Face Teal ▪ #4051

ESTIMATED PRODUCTION: 10,000

STATUS: Retired, 1-7-96

INTRODUCED: 1995 ▪ BIRTHDAY: Unknown

HANG TAG	VALUE 7/1/97	VALUE 1/1/98	VALUE 7/1/98
1ST Generation	–	–	–
2ND Generation	$500	$1,200	$2,450
3RD Generation	$400	$1,200	$2,350
4TH Generation	–	–	–
5TH Generation	–	–	–

*Trademark or name of Ty, Inc., McDonald's Corporation or other distributors of Ty, Inc. dolls, not affiliated with the authors or Schroeder Publishing.

TEDDY*

Old Face Violet ▪ #4055

ESTIMATED PRODUCTION: 15,000

STATUS: Retired, 1-7-95

INTRODUCED: 1994 ▪ BIRTHDAY: Unknown

HANG TAG	VALUE 7/1/97	VALUE 1/1/98	VALUE 7/1/98
1ST Generation	$400	$1,100	$2,400
2ND Generation	$300	$1,100	$2,300
3RD Generation	–	–	–
4TH Generation	–	–	–
5TH Generation	–	–	–

*Trademark or name of Ty, Inc., McDonald's Corporation or other distributors of Ty, Inc. dolls, not affiliated with the authors or Schroeder Publishing.

Although the new face violet Teddy may be the hardest new face to find, the old face violet Teddy may be the easiest old face to locate. The value of this Beanie Baby* isn't less than the other old faces, except brown, but if you are starting a Teddy set he is likely to be one of the first ones you'll find.

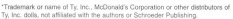

 **BEANIE**

Rx

The new face violet Teddy is often considered the rarest of the new face bears. He comes with a green ribbon around his neck, much like the one new face cranberry has.

TEDDY*

New Face Violet ▪ #4055

ESTIMATED PRODUCTION: 10,000

STATUS: Retired, 1-7-96

INTRODUCED: 1995 ▪ BIRTHDAY: Unknown

HANG TAG	VALUE 7/1/97	VALUE 1/1/98	VALUE 7/1/98
1ST Generation	–	–	–
2ND Generation	$500	$1,200	$2,550
3RD Generation	$400	$1,200	$2,450
4TH Generation	–	–	–
5TH Generation	–	–	–

*Trademark or name of Ty, Inc., McDonald's Corporation or other distributors of Ty, Inc. dolls, not affiliated with the authors or Schroeder Publishing.

TEDDY *

Violet Employee Bear —
Green Ribbon

ESTIMATED PRODUCTION: 200

STATUS: Special Limited Production

INTRODUCED: December 1996 ▪ BIRTHDAY: Unknown

VALUE 7/1/97	VALUE 1/1/98	VALUE 7/1/98
$2,000	$3,500	$5,000

*Trademark or name of Ty, Inc., McDonald's Corporation or other distributors of Ty, Inc. dolls, not affiliated with the authors or Schroeder Publishing.

R

At a Christmas 1996 party to honor its employees and representatives, Ty Inc.* presented each person with this special new face violet Teddy. When the guests arrived for dinner, a bear sat at each place setting. These bears differed from the original new face violets. The Employee Bears had either a green or red ribbon. They didn't have hang tags. Their tush tag was red and white with no name.

Rx

(See information on previous page.)

To tell if the Beanie Baby* is a true Employee Bear or if it is a new face violet Teddy, check the stitching. The Employee Bears were sewn with magenta threading. These Beanie Babies* were made by hand and often have obvious inconsistencies. Their ears are often different sizes. All of the Employee Bears are very plump and have much more filling than a typical Beanie Baby*. Expect these two Employee Bears to become the most sought-after Beanie Babies* in Beanie Baby* history.

TEDDY*

Violet Employee Bear — Red Ribbon

ESTIMATED PRODUCTION: 200
STATUS: Special Limited Production
INTRODUCED: December 1996 ▪ BIRTHDAY: Unknown

VALUE 7/1/97	VALUE 1/1/98	VALUE 7/1/98
$2,000	$3,500	$5,000

97 TEDDY *

The Holiday Bear ▪ #4200

ESTIMATED PRODUCTION: 150,000

STATUS: Retired, 1-1-98

INTRODUCED: 10-1-97 ▪ BIRTHDAY: 12-25-96

Rx

97 Teddy was produced for only two short months in November and December of 1997. Not many 97 Teddys were produced. As soon as supplies of him start diminishing, expect his price to go up considerably. Will there be a 98 or 99 Teddy?

HANG TAG	VALUE 7/1/97	VALUE 1/1/98	VALUE 7/1/98
1ST Generation	–	–	–
2ND Generation	–	–	–
3RD Generation	–	–	–
4TH Generation	–	$35	$60
5TH Generation	–	–	–

*Trademark or name of Ty, Inc., McDonald's Corporation or other distributors of Ty, Inc. dolls, not affiliated with the authors or Schroeder Publishing.

R̲x

TRACKER*

The Basset Hound ▪ #4198

ESTIMATED RETIREMENT: 2000

STATUS: Current

INTRODUCED: 5-30-98 ▪ BIRTHDAY: 6-5-97

"Adorable" best describes the nineteenth dog to the Beanie Baby* family. He was instantly the most popular Beanie Baby* dog. His eyes say buy me and take me home.

HANG TAG	VALUE 7/1/97	VALUE 1/1/98	VALUE 7/1/98
1ST Generation	–	–	–
2ND Generation	–	–	–
3RD Generation	–	–	–
4TH Generation	–	–	–
5TH Generation	–	–	$20

*Trademark or name of Ty, Inc., McDonald's Corporation or other distributors of Ty, Inc. dolls, not affiliated with the authors or Schroeder Publishing.

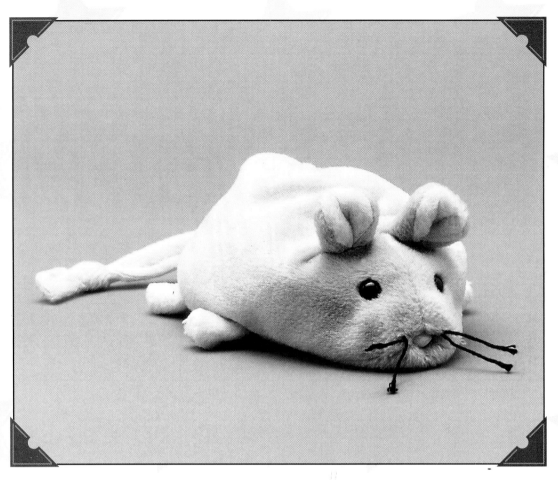

TRAP *

The Mouse ▪ #4042

ESTIMATED PRODUCTION: 35,000

STATUS: Retired, 6-15-95

INTRODUCED: 1994 ▪ BIRTHDAY: Unknown

HANG TAG	VALUE 7/1/97	VALUE 1/1/98	VALUE 7/1/98
1ST Generation	$400	$750	$1,700
2ND Generation	$300	$725	$1,650
3RD Generation	$300	$700	$1,600
4TH Generation	–	–	–
5TH Generation	–	–	–

*Trademark or name of Ty, Inc., McDonald's Corporation or other distributors of Ty, Inc. dolls, not affiliated with the authors or Schroeder Publishing.

DR. BEANIE

Rx

Trap the Mouse was introduced in mid-1994. He doubled in value during the Beanie Baby* craze of December 1996 and January of 1997. He is very difficult to locate and is even harder to find in mint condition. He was retired in 1995. Trap is one of the smallest Beanie Babies*.

DR. BEANIE

Rx

Tuffy is one of the five napped Beanie Babies*. Two of them, Scottie and Tuffy, are terriers. Tuffy and Scottie have the exact same body style.

TUFFY*

The Terrier ▪ #4108

ESTIMATED RETIREMENT: 2000
STATUS: Current

INTRODUCED: 5-11-97 ▪ BIRTHDAY: 1-14-97

HANG TAG	VALUE 7/1/97	VALUE 1/1/98	VALUE 7/1/98
1ST Generation	–	–	–
2ND Generation	–	–	–
3RD Generation	–	–	–
4TH Generation	$10	$10	$10
5TH Generation	–	–	$10

TUSK *

The Walrus ▪ #4076

ESTIMATED PRODUCTION: 100,000
STATUS: Retired, 1-1-97
INTRODUCED: 1996 ▪ BIRTHDAY: 9-18-95

HANG TAG	VALUE 7/1/97	VALUE 1/1/98	VALUE 7/1/98
1ST Generation	–	–	–
2ND Generation	–	–	–
3RD Generation	$40	$110	$255
4TH Generation	$35	$75	$185
5TH Generation	–	–	–

*Trademark or name of Ty, Inc., McDonald's Corporation or other distributors of
Ty, Inc. dolls, not affiliated with the authors or Schroeder Publishing.

Tusk the Walrus was introduced in 1996. Most versions
of Tusk have his tusks facing
down and back. Some versions
of Tusk have the tusks facing
up and forward. Most of
these rarer version Tusks
come with 3rd generation
hang tags. Tusk's name was
also misspelled for a short
while. "Tuck" is a popular variation with collectors.
See the Mistakes and Oddities
Section on page 257 of this
book for Tuck information.

R̲x

Twigs is the only giraffe in the Beanie Baby* family. He is a favorite of young children. His material was also used for the belly of the retired blue Lizzy. Twigs proved to be a popular 1998 McDonald's* Teenie Beanie*.

TWIGS*

The Giraffe ▪ #4068

ESTIMATED PRODUCTION: 3,500,000
STATUS: Retired, 5-1-98
INTRODUCED: 1996 ▪ BIRTHDAY: 5-19-95

HANG TAG	VALUE 7/1/97	VALUE 1/1/98	VALUE 7/1/98
1ST Generation	–	–	–
2ND Generation	–	–	–
3RD Generation	$25	$45	$125
4TH Generation	$10	$10	$25
5TH Generation	–	–	$25

*Trademark or name of Ty, Inc., McDonald's Corporation or other distributors of Ty, Inc. dolls, not affiliated with the authors or Schroeder Publishing.

VALENTINO *

The Bear ▪ #4058

ESTIMATED RETIREMENT: 1999
STATUS: Current
INTRODUCED: 1995 ▪ BIRTHDAY: 2-14-94

HANG TAG	VALUE 7/1/97	VALUE 1/1/98	VALUE 7/1/98
1ST Generation	–	–	–
2ND Generation	–	$115	$250
3RD Generation	–	$70	$130
4TH Generation	–	$20	$18
5TH Generation	–	–	$18

Valentino, a great choice for collectors, is sure to appreciate in value once he retires. Near Valentine's Day he usually goes up in value.
Valentino was used for a Yankee's promotion, a special Toys for Tots fundraising promotion, and a Fannie May* candy promotion. See the Promotion Section of this book for details. Also see page 263 for a Valentino prototype.

Rx

Velvet was very plentiful after her retirement. She is finally starting to grow in value and should continue doing so. Will any more wild cats be entering the Beanie Baby* family soon?

VELVET*

The Panther ▪ #4064

ESTIMATED PRODUCTION: 2,500,000

STATUS: Retired, 10-1-97

INTRODUCED: 1995 ▪ BIRTHDAY: 12-16-95

HANG TAG	VALUE 7/1/97	VALUE 1/1/98	VALUE 7/1/98
1ST Generation	–	–	–
2ND Generation	–	–	–
3RD Generation	$20	$60	$125
4TH Generation	$10	$20	$35
5TH Generation	–	–	–

*Trademark or name of Ty, Inc., McDonald's Corporation or other distributors of Ty, Inc. dolls, not affiliated with the authors or Schroeder Publishing.

WADDLE*

The Penguin • #4075

ESTIMATED PRODUCTION: 3,500,000

STATUS: Retired, 5-1-98

INTRODUCED: 1995 • BIRTHDAY: 12-19-95

Rx

Waddle was introduced in 1995 and can be found with 3rd, 4th, and 5th generation hang tags. One has to wonder why he didn't retire when his close relative Puffer the Puffin was introduced. Ty Inc.* instead retired Waddle May 1, 1998.

HANG TAG	VALUE 7/1/97	VALUE 1/1/98	VALUE 7/1/98
1ST Generation	–	–	–
2ND Generation	–	–	–
3RD Generation	$20	$45	$120
4TH Generation	$10	$10	$25
5TH Generation	–	–	$25

 **Dr. BEANIE**

Rx

Waves' and Echo's tags were reversed when first released. Waves is one of two whales in the Beanie Baby* family. He is basically a sit-up version of Splash.

 # WAVES*

The Whale ▪ #4084

ESTIMATED PRODUCTION: 3,500,000
STATUS: Retired, 5-1-98
INTRODUCED: 5-11-97 ▪ BIRTHDAY: 12-8-96

HANG TAG	VALUE 7/1/97	VALUE 1/1/98	VALUE 7/1/98
1ST Generation	–	–	–
2ND Generation	–	–	–
3RD Generation	–	–	–
4TH Generation	$10	$10	$30
5TH Generation	–	–	$30

WEB*

The Spider ▪ #4041

ESTIMATED PRODUCTION: 35,000

STATUS: Retired, 1-7-96

INTRODUCED: 1994 ▪ BIRTHDAY: Unknown

Web was introduced in mid-1994. He is a very rare Beanie Baby* and his price continues to rise. Get a hold of Web if you can shell out the big bucks. Web was retired in 1996.

HANG TAG	VALUE 7/1/97	VALUE 1/1/98	VALUE 7/1/98
1ST Generation	$400	$850	$1,975
2ND Generation	$355	$825	$1,975
3RD Generation	$325	$780	$1,900
4TH Generation	–	–	–
5TH Generation	–	–	–

*Trademark or name of Ty, Inc., McDonald's Corporation or other distributors of Ty, Inc. dolls, not affiliated with the authors or Schroeder Publishing.

Dr. BEANIE

Rx

Weenie was a great addition to the Beanie Baby* dog family. Weenie can be found with 3rd, 4th, and 5th generation hang tags.

WEENIE*

The Dachshund ▪ #4013

ESTIMATED PRODUCTION: 3,000,000

STATUS: Retired, 5-1-98

INTRODUCED: 1996 ▪ BIRTHDAY: 7-20-95

HANG TAG	VALUE 7/1/97	VALUE 1/1/98	VALUE 7/1/98
1ST Generation	–	–	–
2ND Generation	–	–	–
3RD Generation	$20	$45	$125
4TH Generation	$10	$10	$30
5TH Generation	–	–	$30

WHISPER*

The Deer ▪ #4194

ESTIMATED RETIREMENT: 2004
STATUS: Current
INTRODUCED: 5-30-98 ▪ BIRTHDAY: 4-5-97

Whisper the Deer made a quiet entrance into the Beanie Baby* family. She should prove to be a popular Beanie Baby*. Whisper is the first deer in the Beanie Baby* family.

HANG TAG	VALUE 7/1/97	VALUE 1/1/98	VALUE 7/1/98
1ST Generation	–	–	–
2ND Generation	–	–	–
3RD Generation	–	–	–
4TH Generation	–	–	–
5TH Generation	–	–	$20

 **BEANIE**

Rx

Wise the Owl has a graduation mortar board that says "Class of '98." He is sure to be very collectible. Will there be a Beanie Baby* for the Class of '99? The only problem with Wise is that he was released after high schools' and colleges' "Classes of '98" already graduated. Hopefully if Ty Inc.* comes out with a Class of '99 Beanie Baby* next year, they will make sure to get it out in time.

WISE*

The Owl ▪ #4187

ESTIMATED RETIREMENT: 1999

STATUS: Current

INTRODUCED: 5-30-98 ▪ BIRTHDAY: 5-31-97

HANG TAG	VALUE 7/1/97	VALUE 1/1/98	VALUE 7/1/98
1ST Generation	–	–	–
2ND Generation	–	–	–
3RD Generation	–	–	–
4TH Generation	–	–	–
5TH Generation	–	–	$40

WRINKLES*

The Dog ▪ #4103

ESTIMATED RETIREMENT: 2001

STATUS: Current

INTRODUCED: 1996 ▪ BIRTHDAY: 5-1-96

R

Wrinkles looks much like Pugsly. Wrinkles is easier to come by and will probably be around when Pugsly retires.

HANG TAG	VALUE 7/1/97	VALUE 1/1/98	VALUE 7/1/98
1ST Generation	–	–	–
2ND Generation	–	–	–
3RD Generation	–	–	–
4TH Generation	$10	$10	$10
5TH Generation	–	–	$10

Rx

Ziggy was a surprise retirement in May 1998. Before his retirement, collectors began noticing a different fabric on some Ziggys. This new fabric had stripes wider and farther apart. See the Oddities Section on page 262 for more information and a photo.

ZIGGY*

The Zebra ▪ #4063

ESTIMATED PRODUCTION: 3,500,000

STATUS: Retired, 5-1-98

INTRODUCED: 1995 ▪ BIRTHDAY: 12-24-95

HANG TAG	VALUE 7/1/97	VALUE 1/1/98	VALUE 7/1/98
1ST Generation	–	–	–
2ND Generation	–	–	–
3RD Generation	$20	$45	$125
4TH Generation	$10	$10	$30
5TH Generation	–	–	$30

ZIP *

The Black Cat with White Face and Belly ▪ #4004

ESTIMATED PRODUCTION: 55,000

STATUS: Retired, 1995

INTRODUCED: 1995 ▪ BIRTHDAY: Unknown

HANG TAG	VALUE 7/1/97	VALUE 1/1/98	VALUE 7/1/98
1ST Generation	–	–	–
2ND Generation	$125	$400	$675
3RD Generation	$100	$375	$650
4TH Generation	–	–	–
5TH Generation	–	–	–

Rx

White belly Zip, as he is often referred to, was the first version of Zip produced. He looks much like a kitten. He was introduced at the beginning of 1995. Both his face and belly are white. He was much larger than the Zips that followed. He was redesigned in mid-1995.

Rx

All black Zip is the most valuable of the three Zips. He is not the oldest however. All black Zip was a design change that occurred in mid-1995. His head was made smaller, his body thinner, and he was changed to all black. He looks much different than his predecessor. All black Zip only lasted a few months and was retired in 1996.

ZIP*

The All Black Cat ▪ #4004
ESTIMATED PRODUCTION: 10,000
STATUS: Retired, 3-10-96
INTRODUCED: 1995 ▪ BIRTHDAY: Unknown

HANG TAG	VALUE 7/1/97	VALUE 1/1/98	VALUE 7/1/98
1ST Generation	–	–	–
2ND Generation	–	–	–
3RD Generation	–	$1,400	$2,800
4TH Generation	–	–	–
5TH Generation	–	–	–

ZIP*

The Black Cat with White Paws ▪ #4004

ESTIMATED PRODUCTION: 2,000,000
STATUS: Retired, 5-1-98
INTRODUCED: 1996 ▪ BIRTHDAY: 3-28-94

HANG TAG	VALUE 7/1/97	VALUE 1/1/98	VALUE 7/1/98
1ST Generation	–	–	–
2ND Generation	–	–	–
3RD Generation	–	$300	$625
4TH Generation	$10	$10	$60
5TH Generation	–	–	$60

Zip with white paws is the third version of Zip produced. Zip was a popular Beanie Baby* and was difficult to locate on retail shelves. Zip was nowhere to be seen the two months before his retirement. This sent his value up even before he retired. Expect Zip's value to skyrocket.

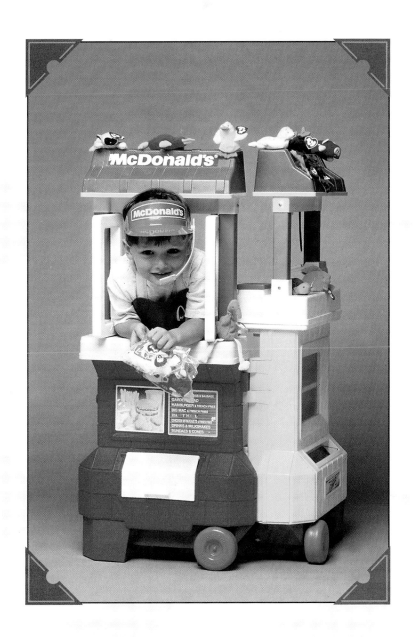

McDonald's*
Teenie Beanies*

McDonald's*
Teenie Beanies*

1997

Friday, April 11, 1997, was a day that will go down in Beanie Baby* history. The McDonald's* Teenie Beanie* Happy Meal* promotion began. Over 100 million Beanie Babies* were produced in ten different styles. McDonald's* planned to release two Teenie Beanies* each week of the five week promotion.

The order of scheduled release was:

No. 1 **Patty the Platypus**
No. 2 **Pinky the Flamingo**

No. 3 **Chops the Lamb**
No. 4 **Chocolate the Moose**

No. 5 **Goldie the Goldfish**
No. 6 **Speedy the Turtle**

No. 7 **Seamore the Seal**
No. 8 **Snort the Bull**

No. 9 **Quacks the Duck**
No. 10 **Lizz the Lizard**

Each Teenie Beanie* style matched an existing Ty Beanie Baby*. Quacks and Lizz were the only name differences. Each Teenie Beanie* came in a clear plastic bag and had a paper heart Ty* hang tag as well as a tush tag. Suggested values in this book are mint in the package (MIP). The Teenie Beanies* exploded onto the market and the demand caught everyone by surprise. The first day, many McDonald's* ran out of their entire week's supply of Beanie Babies*. On April 25, only two weeks into the promotion, McDonald's* formally announced that the promotion would end.

1998

Much to the delight of Beanie Baby* collectors, McDonald's* began their second Teenie Beanie* promotion on May 22, 1998.

The following Teenie Beanies* were featured.

No. 1 **Doby the Doberman**
No. 2 **Bongo the Monkey**

No. 3 **Twigs the Giraffe**
No. 4 **Inch the Worm**

No. 5 **Pinchers the Lobster**
No. 6 **Happy the Hippo**

No. 7 **Mel the Koala**
No. 8 **Scoop the Pelican**

No. 9 **Bones the Dog**
No. 10 **Zip the Cat**

No. 11 **Waddle the Penguin**
No. 12 **Peanut the Elephant**

Again, demand was high but this time McDonald's* and Ty* anticipated the popularity and were better prepared. At least 240 million Teenie Beanies* were produced, still McDonald's* ran out of Beanie Babies* in record time. New collectors now wanted the original 1997 set. This caused a rapid jump in value for the 1997 McDonald's* Teenie Beanies*.

1997 McDonald's* Teenie Beanies*

Patti the Platypus, Pinky the Flamingo, Chops the Lamb, Chocolate the Moose,
Goldie the Goldfish, Speedy the Turtle, Seamore the Seal, Snort the Bull,
Quacks the Duck, and Lizz the Lizard.

VALUE 7/1/97	VALUE 1/1/98	VALUE 7/1/98
$50	$90	$300

PATTI*

The Platypus

· · · · · · · · · ·

VALUE 7/1/97	VALUE 1/1/98	VALUE 7/1/98
$6	$10	$45

*Trademark or name of Ty, Inc., McDonald's Corporation or other distributors of Ty, Inc. dolls, not affiliated with the authors or Schroeder Publishing.

PINKY*

The Flamingo

· · · · · · · · · ·

VALUE 7/1/97	VALUE 1/1/98	VALUE 7/1/98
$8	$15	$55

CHOPS*
The Lamb

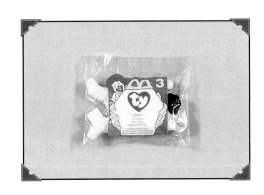

VALUE 7/1/97	VALUE 1/1/98	VALUE 7/1/98
$4	$12	$35

CHOCOLATE*
The Moose

VALUE 7/1/97	VALUE 1/1/98	VALUE 7/1/98
$4	$8	$35

GOLDIE*

The Goldfish

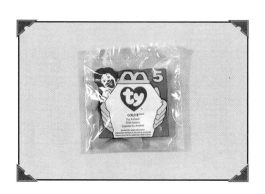

VALUE 7/1/97	VALUE 1/1/98	VALUE 7/1/98
$4	$8	$20

SPEEDY*

The Turtle

VALUE 7/1/97	VALUE 1/1/98	VALUE 7/1/98
$4	$8	$25

SEAMORE*

The Seal

VALUE 7/1/97	VALUE 1/1/98	VALUE 7/1/98
$4	$10	$40

*Trademark or name of Ty, Inc., McDonald's Corporation or other distributors of Ty, Inc. dolls, not affiliated with the authors or Schroeder Publishing.

SNORT*

The Bull

VALUE 7/1/97	VALUE 1/1/98	VALUE 7/1/98
$4	$6	$15

QUACKS*
The Duck

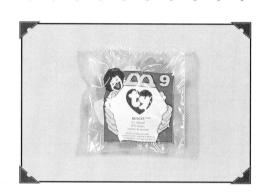

VALUE 7/1/97	VALUE 1/1/98	VALUE 7/1/98
$4	$6	$15

*Trademark or name of Ty, Inc., McDonald's Corporation or other distributors of Ty, Inc. dolls, not affiliated with the authors or Schroeder Publishing.

LIZZ*
The Lizard

VALUE 7/1/97	VALUE 1/1/98	VALUE 7/1/98
$4	$6	$20

1997 McDonald's* Teenie Beanie* Happy Meal* Display

VALUE 7/1/97	VALUE 1/1/98	VALUE 7/1/98
$75	$350	$650

Each McDonald's* restaurant received one display. This cardboard display featured one each of the 10 Teenie Beanies*.

*Trademark or name of Ty, Inc., McDonald's Corporation or other distributors of Ty, Inc. dolls, not affiliated with the authors or Schroeder Publishing.

1997 McDonald's* Teenie Beanie* Happy Meal* Bags

VALUE 7/1/97	VALUE 1/1/98	VALUE 7/1/98
$2 EACH	$20 EACH	$20 EACH

Two different bags were used for the 1997 promotion.

1997 McDonald's* Teenie Beanie*
PROMOTIONAL MATERIAL

1997 McDonald's* Happy Meal* Teenie Beanie Babies* Media Kit

The media kit was distributed to network television executives as a promotion. The box, measuring 13" x 10" x 4" contained 10 compartments. Each compartment held one Teenie Beanie*. One each of the 10 Teenie Beanies* were included with the media kit (unwrapped). Only 250 Media Kits were produced.

VALUE 7/1/97	VALUE 1/1/98	VALUE 7/1/98
$100	$750	$1,800

*Trademark or name of Ty, Inc., McDonald's Corporation or other distributors of Ty, Inc. dolls, not affiliated with the authors or Schroeder Publishing.

1997 McDonald's* Ty* Beanie Babies* Sweepstakes Display

This promotion was optional to McDonald's* restaurants. For a cost of $150.00, the display with 77 Beanie Babies* (regular size) could be purchased. This large display measures 73" in height with a width of 22" and depth of 10".

The McDonald's* that participated held a drawing to win the display and Beanie Babies*. Now, many of these Beanie Babies* have retired.

VALUE 7/1/97	VALUE 1/1/98	VALUE 7/1/98
$500	$1,800	$5,000

1998 McDonald's* Teenie Beanies*

1998 McDonald's* Teenie Beanies*

Doby the Doberman, Bongo the Monkey, Twigs the Giraffe, Inch the Worm,
Pinchers the Lobster, Happy the Hippo, Mel the Koala, Scoop the Pelican,
Bones the Dog, Zip the Cat, Waddle the Penguin, and Peanut the Elephant.

12 BAG SET
VALUE 7/1/98
$100

DOBY*

The Doberman

VALUE 7/1/98

$17

*Trademark or name of Ty, Inc., McDonald's Corporation or other distributors of Ty, Inc. dolls, not affiliated with the authors or Schroeder Publishing.

BONGO*

The Monkey

VALUE 7/1/98

$20

TWIGS*

The Giraffe

VALUE 7/1/98

$18

*Trademark or name of Ty, Inc., McDonald's Corporation or other distributors of Ty, Inc. dolls, not affiliated with the authors or Schroeder Publishing.

INCH*

The Worm

VALUE 7/1/98

$5

PINCHERS*

The Lobster

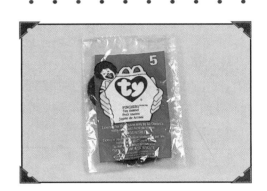

VALUE 7/1/98
$6

HAPPY*

The Hippo

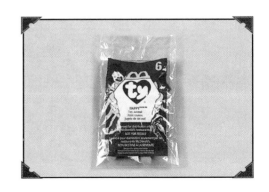

VALUE 7/1/98
$7

MEL*

The Koala

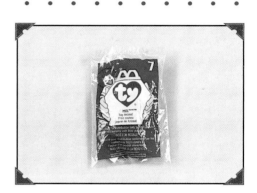

VALUE 7/1/98
$8

SCOOP*

The Pelican

VALUE 7/1/98
$9

BONES*

The Dog

VALUE 7/1/98
$10

ZIP*

The Cat

VALUE 7/1/98
$12

WADDLE*

The Penguin

VALUE 7/1/98

$12

PEANUT*

The Elephant

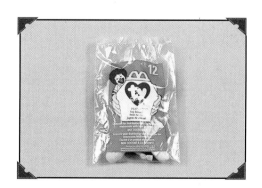

VALUE 7/1/98

$11

1998 McDonald's* Teenie Beanie*
PROMOTIONAL MATERIAL

1998 McDONALD'S* TEENIE BEANIE* HAPPY MEAL* DISPLAY

Each McDonald's* restaurant received one display. This cardboard display featured one each of the 12 Teenie Beanies*.

VALUE 7/1/98
$300

WINDOW DISPLAY

These signs were hung in McDonald's* windows with suction cups to announce which Teenie Beanies* were currently being distributed. Approximately 13 inches in length, there was one sign for each Teenie Beanie*.

VALUE 7/1/98
SET OF 12
$240

220

1998 McDonald's* Teenie Beanie*
PROMOTIONAL MATERIAL

1998 McDonald's* Teenie Beanie* Pins

Set of 12 gold clutch pins. On back of pins is written: "Group II, China."

VALUE 7/1/98
SET OF 12
$300

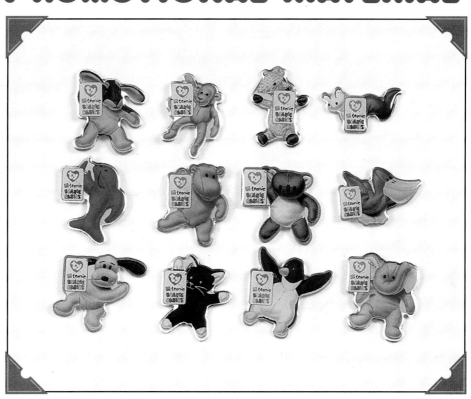

McDonald's* Employee Button

VALUE 7/1/98
$25

McDonald's* Employee Shirt And Cap

VALUE 7/1/98
$100
PER SET

221

1998 McDonald's* Teenie Beanie*
PROMOTIONAL MATERIAL

1998 McDonald's* Teenie Beanie* Happy Meal* Bags

Two different bags were used for the 1998 promotion.

VALUE 7/1/98

$5
EACH

1998 McDonald's* Teenie Beanie* Happy Meal* Test Bag Set

The rare McDonald's* Teenie Beanie* test issue bags were distributed in the city of Colorado Springs and the city of Albuquerque, New Mexico. Each bag has a small paper insert with Ronald McDonald's picture which counted toward a redemption program for CDs and other prizes.

VALUE 7/1/98

SET OF 12
$200

McDonald's* Teenie Beanie* Hang Tags

Hang tags were attached with red thread.

1997, 1998   1997   1998

McDonald's* Teenie Beanie* Tush Tags

Teenie Beanies* were manufactured by two companies: Simon Marketing, Inc. and M.B. Sales. Canadian Teenie Beanies* have a larger tush tag in both English and French.

The Carey clan ate their fair share of hamburgers!

BEANIE BABY*
PROMOTIONS

Beanie Babies* have been used to promote everything. Some promotions have been endorsed by Ty Inc.* while others were not endorsed. The first promotion was with the Chicago Cubs. Promotions at other sporting events have been endless. Beanie Babies* have been used to raise money for schools, charities, hospitals, and other organizations. They have been used to promote books, sell jewelry, and even doll clothes.

Where will it end? The better question is "where will it go?"

As long as the public desires these loveable toys,
the promotions will continue...with success.

BEANIE BABY*
SPORTS PROMOTIONS

It all started on a historical day at Wrigley Field in Chicago. On May 18, 1997, the Chicago Cubs and Ty Inc.* hosted Beanie Baby* Day. The first 10,000 children age 13 and under received Cubbie the brown bear and a commemorative card with admission to the game. Early in the day, the lines started to form as the crowds waited anxiously to get their Cubbie. The children were thrilled and a sea of Cubbies waved in their hands in the stands during the game. H. Ty Warner, founder of Ty Inc.*, threw out the first pitch of the game.

Little did Ty know this would be the first of many sports promotions. The Cubs repeated the promotion on September 6, 1997. Since then, many sports teams have had a Beanie Babies* game or plan to have one.

1998 promotions are also planned by teams in the Women's National Basketball Association, the National Hockey League, and the National Football League.

The following list includes some of the sport promotions:

EVENT	DATE	BEANIE	# PRODUCED
Chicago Cubs	May 18, 1997	Cubbie	10,000
Chicago Cubs	Sept. 6, 1997	Cubbie	10,000
Chicago Cubs	Jan. 1998	Cubbie	100
Philadelphia 76ers	Jan. 17, 1998	Baldy	5,000
N.Y. Yankees—Spring Training	Mar. 10, 1998	Bones	5,000
San Antonio Spurs	Mar. 1998	Curly	2,500
San Antonio Spurs	Mar. 1998	Pinky	2,500
Oakland A's—Spring Training	Mar. 15, 1998	Ears	1,500
Indiana Pacers	April 2, 1998	Strut	5,000
Cleveland Cavaliers	April 4, 1998	Bongo	5,000
Denver Nuggets	April 17, 1998	Chocolate	5,000
Chicago Cubs	May 3, 1998	Daisy	10,000
New York Yankees	May 17, 1998	Valentino	24,000
St. Louis Cardinals	May 22, 1998	Stretch	20,000
Detroit Tigers	May 31, 1998	Stripes	10,000
Kansas City Royals	May 31, 1998	Roary	15,000
Milwaukee Brewers	May 31, 1998	Batty	12,000
Charlotte Sting	June 15, 1998	Curly	5,000
Arizona Diamondbacks	June 14, 1998	Hissy	6,500
Allstar Game	July 7, 1998	Glory	75,000
Washington Mystics	July 11, 1998	Mystic	Unknown
New York Mets	July 12, 1998	Batty	12,000
Chicago White Sox	July 12, 1998	Blizzard	Unknown
Detroit Shock	July 25, 1998	Mel	5,000
Tampa Bay Devil Rays	July 26, 1998	Weenie	15,000
Minnesota Twins	July 31, 1998	Lucky	Unknown
Oakland A's	Aug. 1, 1998	Peanut	15,000
Detroit Tigers	Aug. 8, 1998	Stripes	10,000
New York Yankees	Aug. 9, 1998	Stretch	24,000
St. Louis Cardinals	Aug. 14, 1998	Smoochy	Unknown
Cincinnati Reds	Aug. 16, 1998	Rover	Unknown
Houston Astros	Aug. 16, 1998	Derby	Unknown
Atlanta Braves	Aug. 19, 1998	Chip	Unknown
Chicago Cubs	Sept. 13, 1998	Gracie	Unknown

CUBBIE

Chicago Cubs, May 18, 1997

Presented at Ty Beanie Babies* Day, and sponsored by Pepsi*, the first 10,000 children, 13 and under, were given Cubbie. This Cubbie had a 4th generation tag and no tush tag star. The laminated commemorative card was not numbered. The giveaway was advertised in a full-page ad on April 29 in the Chicago Tribune. The Cubs played the Giants.

VALUE 7/1/98
$375

CUBBIE

Chicago Cubs
September 6, 1997

Also called "Cubbie Goes Back to School," the second Cubs–Ty* promotion was also given to the first 10,000 children, 13 and under. The Cubs played the St. Louis Cardinals. The card is not numbered.

VALUE 7/1/98
$325

CUBBIE'S FIRST CONVENTION

Chicago Cubs, January, 1998

During the Cub's 13th Annual Chicago Cubs Convention in January 1998, 100 special convention Cubbies were raffled off. These Cubbies had a special laminated card.
The card is not numbered.

VALUE 7/1/98
$800

*Trademark or name of Ty, Inc., McDonald's Corporation or other distributors of Ty, Inc. dolls, not affiliated with the authors or Schroeder Publishing.

BALDY

Philadelphia 76ers
January 17, 1998

The 76ers were the first NBA team to sponsor a Beanie Babies* day. Approximately 5,000 Baldys with laminated cards were presented to children. The cards were numbered. The 76ers played the Golden State Warriors.

VALUE 7/1/98
$300

BONES

With Card

**New York Yankees
vs.
Toronto Bluejays
March 10, 1998**

VALUE 7/1/98
$250

Bones was presented to all children 14 and under along with an unnumbered commemorative card at Legends Field, Tampa, Florida. Many of the 5,000 Beanie Babies* and cards were not given out since it was a school night and the stands were full of adult season ticket holders. It was a freezing night in Florida, but the Careys and friends enjoyed the fun!

Tara Carey with Bones

Kyle Carey,
Tara Carey,
Mary D'Angelo,
Megan Carey,
Lindsay Hatcher,
and Kelly Carey

CURLY AND PINKY

San Antonio Spurs
Curly, April 27, 1998 and
Pinky, April 29, 1998

The San Antonio Spurs had two Beanie Babies* nights. On April 27, 1998, Curly was distributed and on April 29, 1998, Pinky was the Beanie Baby* presented. Both nights, 2,500 Beanie Babies* and cards were given to children 14 and under.
All cards were numbered.

VALUE 7/1/98
$200 Each

*Trademark or name of Ty, Inc., McDonald's Corporation or other distributors of Ty, Inc. dolls, not affiliated with the authors or Schroeder Publishing.

EARS

Oakland A's, Spring Training,
March 15, 1998

Oakland A's Ears was presented to children at Phoenix Municipal Stadium. The A's played the Anaheim Angels for Beanie Babies* Day. Many collectors don't know about this commemorative day so expect the Ears and card to appreciate in value. The card is a thin material and is not numbered.

VALUE 7/1/98
$325

STRUT

**Indiana Pacers,
April 2, 1998**

5,000 Struts with commemorative cards
were presented to young fans
on April 2, 1998.

VALUE 7/1/98

$200

BONGO

Cleveland Cavaliers, April 4, 1998

Beanie Babies* Day at Gund Arena featured Bongo
with a numbered commemorative card. 5,000 fans,
age 12 and under, received Bongo and watched
the Cavaliers play the L.A. Clippers.

VALUE 7/1/98

$200

CHOCOLATE

**Denver Nuggets,
April 17, 1998**

Denver Nuggets presented Chocolate the Moose, and a numbered commemorative card to all children, 18 and under. At the gate all children received a redemption slip which was exchanged for Chocolate at one of several inside distribution booths.
Denver played the Portland Trailblazers for their last game of the season.

VALUE 7/1/98
$300

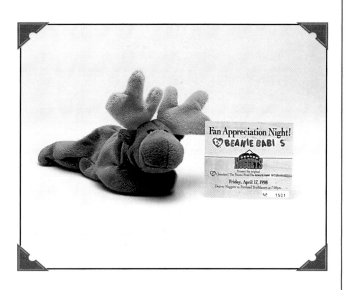

• • • • • • • • • • • •

Commemorative cards presented with Chocolate.

Kelly Carey enjoying the game.

Kyle Carey receiving his Chocolate.

*Trademark or name of Ty, Inc., McDonald's Corporation or other distributors of Ty, Inc. dolls, not affiliated with the authors or Schroeder Publishing.

PROMOTIONS

"HOLY COW!"

Chicago Cubs, May 3, 1998

In tribute to the Chicago Cubs announcer Harry Caray, who died February 18, 1998, Ty Inc.* and the Cubs held another Beanie Baby* promotion. On Sunday, May 3, 1998, Daisy the Cow was presented to 10,000 children, age 13 and under, at Wrigley Field. These Daisys had a special hang tag. The inside of the tag had a caricature of Harry Caray. Included on the tag was a special poem in honor of Mr. Caray. The commemorative cards were not numbered.

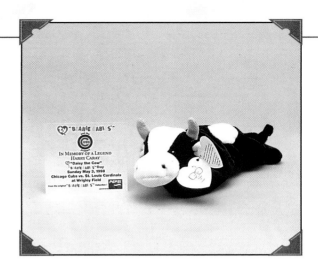

VALUE 7/1/98
$600

VALENTINO

New York Yankees, May 17, 1998

New York Yankees played the Minnesota Twins on Beanie Babies* Day. Approximately 24,000 Valentinos were distributed with a numbered commemorative card. David Wells pitched a perfect game. A Valentino and card were sent to the Baseball Hall of Fame, Cooperstown.

VALUE 7/1/98
$250

STRETCH

St. Louis Cardinals, May 22, 1998

The Cardinals played the San Francisco Giants at Busch Stadium for Beanie Babies* night. Stretch was given out to 20,000 children, 15 and under. The cards were not numbered.

VALUE 7/1/98
$200

232

STRIPES

Detroit Tigers, May 31, 1998

Stripes had already retired when it was presented to 10,000 children, 14 and under, which made it a very popular promotion. The Tigers played the Chicago White Sox at Tiger Stadium. The collector cards were not numbered.

VALUE 7/1/98
$200

ROARY

Kansas City Royals, May 31, 1998

Kansas City Royals played the Oakland A's on Beanie Day* at Kauffman Stadium. 15,000 numbered cards and Roarys were distributed that night.

VALUE 7/1/98
$200

BATTY

Milwaukee Brewers, May 31, 1998

12,000 Battys were presented to children on Beanies Babies* Day. These cards were not numbered.

VALUE 7/1/98
$200

HISSY

Arizona Diamondbacks, June 14, 1998

Only 6,500 Hissys were presented to children on Beanie Babies* Day. This Hissy with card should appreciate in value due to the limited supply. The collector card was not numbered and the paper stock is thin.

VALUE 7/1/98
$200

Becky Estenssoro, Sara Nelson (Beanie* Mom), Becky Phillips, and Vicky Krupka.

"Show Me The Beanies*!"

Collier County Museum, Naples, Florida ▪ December 15, 1997 – January 31, 1998

BEANIE BABIES*
THE FIRST EVER
MUSEUM EXHIBIT

The first ever museum exhibit of Beanie Babies* occured
December 15, 1997 – January 31, 1998
at the Collier County Museum in Naples, Florida.
On January 10, 1998, Beanie Mania authors Becky Phillips and Becky Estenssoro, with
Beanie* Mom, Sara Nelson and Vicky Krupka presented a program on
Beanie Baby* collecting at the nearby Registry Hotel.

Tara Carey with Beanie Mania
authors Becky and Becky.
Becky Phillips and
Becky Estenssoro.

Christmas 1997
SHOW ME THE BEANIES!
Collier County Museum
Naples, Florida

Ty © does not endorse or have any affiliation with this exhibit

VALUE 7/1/98

$75

Tara Carey gets an autograph from
Vicki Krupa.

BEANIE BABIES*
TOY FAIR CONGO

Toy Fair Congo was a promotion at the February 1998 New York Toy Fair. *Beanie Mania* authors, Becky Phillips and Becky Estenssoro presented a Toy Fair Congo with each purchase of 36 of their books. This Congo had a red velvet ribbon around his neck with the words "1998 New York Toy Fair" stitched in gold.

Included with the Congo was a commemorative card.

These cards were numbered 0001 – 1998, with only 1998 of these card produced.

VALUE 7/1/98
$300

*Trademark or name of Ty, Inc., McDonald's Corporation or other distributors of Ty, Inc. dolls, not affiliated with the authors or Schroeder Publishing.

VALUE 7/1/98

$200 each

BONGO

PINKY

In their February 8, 1998, advertising flyers, Kmart and Service Merchandise offered promotions which included Beanie Babies.* The Service Merchandise promotion offered a "Free Genuine Ty Beanie Baby*" with a purchase of diamond earrings for $49.97. At Kmarts, for $49.99, the customer received a diamond pendant with a Beanie Baby* in a boxed set. **Kmart Corporation agreed to halt the promotion shortly after it began after Ty Inc.* filed a lawsuit for copyright violations against Kmart.**

TOYS FOR TOTS* PROMOTION

In March 1998, Toys for Tots* offered Valentino with a limited edition tag. This tag was a large round tag with the 50th Anniversary for Toys for Tots* logo. These tags were numbered 1 to 5500. Proceeds from the sale of these Valentinos went to the Toys for Tots Foundation*. Included with the Valentino, in addition to the special tag, were a numbered Toys for Tots* certificate and a registration form.

VALUE 7/1/98

$450

VALENTINO

PROMOTIONS

MEGA FUN PACK

FUN PACK

Beckett and Associates produced unauthorized fun packs in 1997. These fun packs were sold in Kmart and Meijer stores in Michigan, Ohio, Illinois, and Indiana.

The Mega Collector's Fun Pack was packaged in a box. The box included one regular sized Beanie Baby*, trading cards, comic book, and pogs. It retailed for $19.99.

The Collector's Fun Pack included one Ty* Teenie Beanie* and two, three, or six packages of trading cards. These fun packs retailed at $5.99–9.99 and were in clear bags.

VALUE 7/1/98	
MEGA COLLECTORS FUN PACK	COLLECTORS FUN PACK
$25 - $90	$15 - $40
Value varies with value of the Beanie in the package.	

BROADWAY BEANIES*

The Broadway production company Livent Inc.* had very successful promotions linking their shows with Beanie Babies*. Each show had several Beanie Babies* which were only sold in their theater gift shops. Each Beanie Baby* had a special ribbon around its neck. All of these Broadway Beanies* were chosen by Livent Inc.* for a specific reason. They tied in with the show, the era, a song lyric or a show color theme. Beanie Babies* were sold at both their U.S. and Canadian productions. The theater shops imposed limits on the purchase of these Broadway Beanies* requiring a ticket stub for purchase. Most collectors desire the ticket stub and program for documentation of the Beanie Baby* since the ribbons were available on other products in the gift shops.

BROADWAY BEANIES*
PHANTOM OF THE OPERA

To Date: Only available in Canada   **VALUE 7/1/98**

Phantom Velvet $100
Chosen for the black and white color scheme.

Phantom Bongo . . . .$ 75
Chosen because there is a monkey music box featured in the show.

Phantom Maple $500
*Chosen because Livent Inc. is a Canadian company. Phantom was its first production
10 years ago.*

Phantom Peanut $100
Chosen because there is a large blue elephant set piece in the show.

*A Phantom mask pin was attached to each ribbon. The red satin ribbon has the Phantom of the
Opera printed on it in gold. Phantom Broadway Beanies* first released did not have the pin.*

BROADWAY BEANIES*
SHOWBOAT

<u>VALUE 7/1/98</u>

Showboat Scoop ....$ 75

Showboat Goldie $100
Both Scoop and Goldie were chosen due to the river location. Also the famous song "Can't Help Lovin' Dat Man" starts with lines "Fish gotta swim, birds gotta fly."

Showboat Valentino $150
Valentino was also chosen because of the song "Can't Help Lovin' Dat Man."

The Showboat ribbon is a light blue satin with Showboat printed in white letters.

BROADWAY BEANIES*
JOSEPH AND THE AMAZING
TECHNICOLOR DREAMCOAT

VALUE 7/1/98

Joseph Garcia $300
Chosen because of their technicolor look.

Joseph Peace $150
Chosen because of their technicolor look.

Joseph Fleece .... $ 75
Chosen because there are sheep in the show.

Joseph Inch $100
Chosen because of their technicolor look.

The ribbon is a rainbow striped grosgrain with no show name printed on it.

For a short time last year, the Canadian theater ran out of Curlys to sell. Ty* didn't have any extra Curlys to send Livent Inc.* but they sent the theater new face brown Teddys instead. The set of the three Teddies is much more valuable than the Curly set.

BROADWAY BEANIES*
RAGTIME

Ragtime Curly — burgundy ribbon

Ragtime Curly — cream ribbon

Ragtime Curly — navy ribbon

VALUE 7/1/98
$450 Per Set

Ragtime Teddy — burgundy ribbon

Ragtime Teddy — cream ribbon

Ragtime Teddy — navy ribbon

VALUE 7/1/98
$700 Per Set

Three different colors of satin ribbon were used. Ragtime was printed in gold letters. Teddy bears were used since the Teddy bear was popular during the Ragtime era. Curly was chosen first because he had an old fashioned look to him.

PROMOTIONS

CANDIDE

FOSSE

BROADWAY BEANIES*
CANDIDE AND FOSSE

Candide — Roary
Chosen because there is a singing lion in the show.

Candide — Fleece
Chosen because there are two singing lambs in the show.

Fosse — Strut
Chosen because the dancers in Fosse strut their stuff.

VALUE 7/1/98
$75 Each
(Candide)

VALUE 7/1/98
$50
(Fosse)

The violet blue satin ribbon is 7/8" wide. All other ribbons are 5/8" in width. Candide is printed in white letters. The red satin ribbon has Fosse printed in black script. The ribbon is tied around Strut's comb like a sweat band.

THE YUKON QUEST

The Yukon Quest is the annual 1000 mile dogsled race in Canada.
As part of the 1998 official memorabilia of the race, Nanook was sold.
This Yukon Quest Nanook has a red ribbon which is printed with "Yukon Quest
The Ultimate Challenge." Proceeds from this promotion go to a fund to aid injured
musher Peter Zimmerman who was hurt in an accident while training.
The cost of this Nanook was $12.95 (Canadian dollars).

VALUE 7/1/98
$50

CHINESE NEW YEAR STRIPES

The 1998 Year of the Tiger was celebrated by the Art House*, in Toronto, Ontario, Canada, with a promotion which included Stripes. The Art House* purchased Stripes directly from Ty Inc.* Proceeds from the sale went to the Asian Seniors Community. The tiger sold for $34.95 (Canadian dollars) and less than 1,000 were produced. The special commemorative red card contained the Canadian 45¢ stamp for the Year of the Tiger. Stripes had a red satin ribbon around his neck with gold Chinese characters embossed on it. Red represents luck and gold represents wealth.

VALUE 7/1/98
$350

FANNIE MAY CANDIES*

Fannie May Candies* has been packaging Beanie Babies*
with their candy for special promotions.

Christmas 1997
Rover was packaged with small chocolates wrapped as Christmas presents. $14.95

Valentines 1998
Valentino was packaged with a clear heart filled with chocolate. When these were quickly sold out a heart of chocolate was used. $19.95

Easter 1998
Hippity was featured in the Carrot Handle Basket promotion. Assorted Easter chocolates were included. $39.95

Spring 1998
Ladybug Love Box — Lucky was packaged with a chocolate sunflower filled with chocolate ladybugs. $24.95

VALUE 7/1/98
$50 Each

SPOT

Madame Alexander Spot
Playdate with Spot,
by Madame Alexander*,
was released fall 1996.
This boxed set included Spot
with clothes for the
Madame Alexander* doll
Little Huggums. It was available
only in exclusive doll shops and
retailed for approximately $45.99.
Each retailer only received a few
Playdate with Spots, therefore
it is extremely rare.

VALUE 7/1/98
$1,200

PRINCESS

The release of Princess the Bear
was exciting and emotional for
Beanie Baby* collectors. Everyone
wanted the bear which would honor
the late Princess Diana. Ty Inc.*
agreed to donate proceeds to the
Princess Diana Fund. Each vendor
was to receive only 12 Princess Bears
in December. It was suggested that
stores hold drawings or raffles for the
bear with profits to be donated to the
Diana, Princess of Wales Memorial Fund.
These original bears have PVC on their
tush tags. In January, many stores
received an additional 36 bears. These
bears have PE on the tush tags. In May
1998, representatives from Ty Inc.* presented a check for $2,004,850.00 to the
fund. This check was for profits realized
by Ty* from the Princess Bear.

VALUE 7/1/98	
PVC $150	PE $50

*Trademark or name of Ty, Inc., McDonald's Corporation or other distributors of Ty, Inc. dolls, not affiliated with the authors or Schroeder Publishing.

1990 Teddy

In the beginning...
Before Beanie Babies*,
Ty Inc.* produced
a line of Teddies.
**This 18" napped Teddy
was produced in 1990.**

Megan Carey with her '90 Teddy.
The Teddy was a baby gift to her.

Nephew Hayden Carey with
his much loved '90 Teddy.
Notice Teddy only has one
eye remaining!

*Trademark or name of Ty, Inc., McDonald's Corporation or other distributors of Ty, Inc. dolls, not affiliated with the authors or Schroeder Publishing.

BEANIE BABIES*
COLLECTING WITH
THE HOLIDAYS

The holiday Beanie Babies* released October 1, 1997, were

Snowball the Snowman, Batty the Bat, Spinner the Spider,

Gobbles the Turkey, and the '97 Teddy.

Snowball the Snowman and the '97 Teddy

were retired January 1, 1998.

VALENTINE WREATH
. . . .

VALENTINE BOX
. . . .

Happy *St. Patrick's Day!*

ST. PATRICK'S SIGN
. . . .

ST. PATRICK'S WREATH
. . . .

EASTER BASKET

. . . .

SPRING DISPLAY

. . . .

*Trademark or name of Ty, Inc., McDonald's Corporation or other distributors of Ty, Inc. dolls, not affiliated with the authors or Schroeder Publishing.

INDEPENDENCE DAY

. . . .

THANKSGIVING DAY

. . . .

HALLOWEEN WREATH

HALLOWEEN PUMPKIN

*Trademark or name of Ty, Inc., McDonald's Corporation or other distributors of Ty, Inc. dolls, not affiliated with the authors or Schroeder Publishing.

CHRISTMAS DISPLAY

CHRISTMAS TREE

BEANIE BABIES*
COLLECTING GROUPS

Many collectors prefer to limit their collections to certain categories of
Beanie Babies*. Included are some of the more popular groups.

BIRDS
· · · · · · · · · · ·

DOGS
· · · · · · · · · · · ·

JUNGLE ANIMALS
· · · · · · · · · · ·

CATS
· · · · · · · · · · · ·

FOREST ANIMALS
. . . .

TEDDY BEARS
. . . .

SEA ANIMALS
. . . .

FARM ANIMALS
. . . .

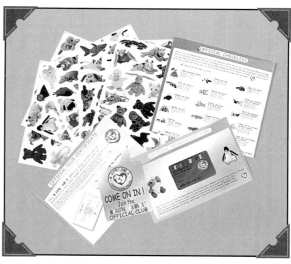

BEANIE BABIES*
OFFICIAL CLUB

At last, what many had been waiting for, an official Beanie Babies* club. Available spring 1998, designated vendors began selling Beanie Babies* Official Club kits for $10.00. Included in the price was a giant poster.

In the box were the following items:

1. **Official Charter Membership Card** — a gold credit-card styled card with an individual number
2. **136 Official Beanie Babies* Stickers** — 4 sheets, to be placed on the poster
3. **Official Beanie Babies* Checklist** — includes a picture of each Beanie*, name, birthday, style number, date issued, and date if retired
4. **Official Beanie Babies* Newsletter**
5. **Certificate of Authenticity Offer** — a postcard to mail in for the certificate
6. **Beanie Babies* Doorknob Hanger**
7. **Sticker Instruction Sheet**
   Ty* then announced that club members would be able to purchase a special limited edition Beanie Baby*, named Clubbie.

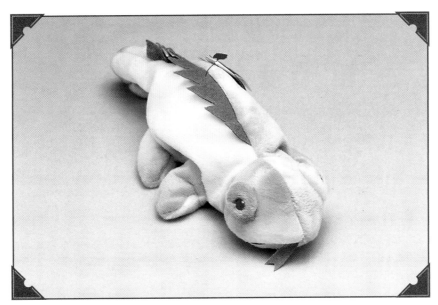

Iggy

with sideways tongue

Beanie Baby*
Mistakes and Oddities

Any product which is mass produced will have some errors. Mistakes do happen. Beanie Babies* have been produced in China, Korea, and Indonesia. Since these countries are non-English speaking, this increases the odds of mistakes, especially the writing on tags. Some mistakes add value to the Beanie*, yet others add no additional value. To most collectors mistakes and oddities add an interesting aspect to Beanie* collecting.

HANG TAG ERRORS

Some Beanie Babies* have been shipped with incorrect hang tags. This mistake generally adds little or no value to the Beanie* since it can be easily duplicated by switching Beanie* hang tags.

Other Beanies* have tags with misspelled poems, names, birthdays, or other hang tag writing. Again, these misprints add little or no value to the Beanie*. Some tags have even been shipped with no writing on the tag.

The Beanie Babies™ Collection

© Ty Inc.
Oakbrook IL. U.S.A.

© Ty UK Ltd.
Waterlooville, Hants
PO8 8HH

© Ty Deutschland
90008 Nürnberg

Handmade in China

Tuck™ style 4076

DATE OF BIRTH : 9-18-95

Tusk brushes his teeth everyday
To keep them shiny, it's the only way
Teeth are special, so they you must try
So they sparkle when You say "Hi"!

Visit our web page!!!

http://www.ty.com

An example of an increase in value with a hang tag error is Snort with a Tabasco hang tag. Since no one in their right Beanie* mind would take a tag off of Tabasco to put on a Snort, it is considered a desirable mistake. These mis-tagged Snorts are valued at about $75.

For a short time in 1996, Tusk the walrus was released with "Tuck" printed on the heart hang tag. This mistake is a great buy at approximately $50 more than the correctly tagged Tusk.

TUSH TAG ERRORS

Many Beanie Babies* have been shipped with incorrect tush tags. Most incorrect tush tags add only a little value to the Beanie*. Some of these Beanies* also have incorrect hang tags. Well known examples of hang and tush tag errors are

Echo and Waves
Sparky with Dotty Tag.

Many collectors feel that Rainbow and Iggy were produced with switched tags. It appears instead that the fabric was accidentally switched at the factory.

One important tush tag error is the Canadian bear, Maple. The first 3000 bears released had the name Pride on their tush tag. Pride was the original name for the bear, but the name was changed to Maple. These 3000 Maple/Pride bears have a Pride tush tag and a Maple hang tag. Maple/Pride currently sells for 2–3 times the price of Maple.

Another tush tag error was found with Libearty. When Libearty the Bear was first released, Beanie* on the tush tag was misspelled as <u>Beanine</u>. Later, the tag was corrected. However, there are fewer correct tags than misspelled tags so the Beanine tag is actually more common. Currently, both

sell for the same amount. It is not uncommon to find tags with incorrectly spelled words. Other common misspellings include the word surface as "surfrace" on 4th generation tush tags and the word original as "oriiginal" on the front of many 5th generation hang tags. These misspellings do not increase the value.

ODDITIES

Oddities are errors in the production of the Beanie*. Oddities include missing, extra, backward, or upside-down parts. Many people collect oddities. Oddities generally add value to the Beanie Baby*. The availability or rarity of the oddity determines the value.

AMERICAN TRIO
with upside down flags

VALUE 7/1/98
$2,000

BONGO
with backward leg

VALUE 7/1/98
$50

*Trademark or name of Ty, Inc., McDonald's Corporation or other distributors of Ty, Inc. dolls, not affiliated with the authors or Schroeder Publishing.

MAPLE
with upside down flag

VALUE 7/1/98
$350

DERBY
with backward ear

VALUE 7/1/98
$50

INKY
with seven legs

VALUE 7/1/98

$250

INKY
with nine legs

VALUE 7/1/98

$250

INKY
with ten legs

VALUE 7/1/98

$400

DAISY
with no spot

VALUE 7/1/98

$175

FRECKLES
with no tail

VALUE 7/1/98
$75

KIWI
with backward wing

VALUE 7/1/98
$250

*Trademark or name of Ty, Inc., McDonald's Corporation or other distributors of Ty, Inc. dolls, not affiliated with the authors or Schroeder Publishing.

STRIPES
fuzzy belly — newer caramel & black tiger

VALUE 7/1/98
$250

LUCKY
½ fabric 21 dot, ½ fabric 7 dot

VALUE 7/1/98
$400

MAPLE

Special Olympics — with upside-down flag

VALUE 7/1/98
$900

BUMBLE

with no antennas

VALUE 7/1/98
$950

*Trademark or name of Ty, Inc., McDonald's Corporation or other distributors of Ty, Inc. dolls, not affiliated with the authors or Schroeder Publishing.

ZIGGY

with different material

VALUE 7/1/98
$50

BLIZZARD

with no tail

VALUE 7/1/98
$75

This prototype of Valentino is smaller in size, has a lighter nose, and the red color of the heart is slightly different. Note the ribbon is also a lighter shade of red. This prototype Valentino was accidentally shipped to a Texas store with their regular order.
(Prototype is on the left.)

BEANIE BABY* PROTOTYPES

Production of a Beanie Baby* is a long process. Often a Beanie* goes through a couple design changes. Different prototypes are made for each prospective Beanie*. The prototypes may differ in shape, fabric, or parts, such as eyes, antennas, or mouths. Once the Beanie* is perfected it is manufactured. Prototypes are usually made in a few different colors, with between one and six of each of these colors produced.

PROTOTYPES

This prototype of Floppity is very similar to the final Floppity version. Prototype Floppity is fatter and has a different ribbon. He also has tags from a company called Pax. This prototype was purchased in a London store. His authenticity was confirmed by Ty* UK Ltd.

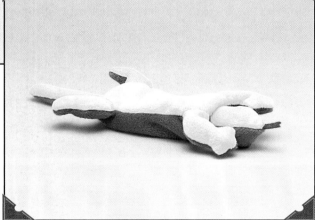

This prototype of Lizzy shows a different fabric. This fabric is a bright blue with a bright yellow body. The body shape is almost identical, but the body is smaller. The tongue is also much shorter.

This prototype Lizzy, along with five others, was obtained in China by an American businessman from one of the factories producing Beanie Babies* for Ty Inc.* Those six are identical and are believed to be the only prototypes of their kind.

• • • • • • • • • • •

BEANIE BABY*
COUNTERFEITS

Unfortunately, any collectible, especially one of value, is subject to unauthorized reproductions. Beanie Babies* are no exception. Counterfeit Beanie Babies* are flooding the market. Most fakes are poorly done and most Beanie* dealers can identify them. However, some counterfeits are well made and difficult to spot.

Buyer beware! If a deal is too good to be true, it probably is! Purchase only from reliable dealers whom you can trust.

Most fakes have done a poor job duplicating the hang tag or the tush tag. Fake tush tags are often larger than an authentic tush tag and the spacing of the type is often different. Counterfeit hang tags often show poorly reproduced gold foil trim on the tag. Also, the font used on the hang tag is often different. In some instances the ink can be rubbed off the fake tag.

Counterfeit fabric tends to be slightly different. Usually it is not as plush. Rubbing the fabric feels different, usually it is not as smooth.

> **Buyer beware! If a deal is too good to be true, it probably is! Purchase only from reliable dealers whom you can trust.**

COUNTERFEITS

The following are some of the counterfeits we have found.
The authentic Beanie Baby* is on the right, the fake on the left.

• •

Princess Bear

The Princess Bear is a very well made counterfeit Beanie Baby*. Some dealers have been fooled by it. When compared to the authentic, the fake Princess is slightly lighter in color and the fabric feels different. The ribbon on the fake Princess is satin on the outside and dull on the inside. The Ty* Princess has a satin finish on both sides. The tags on the fake Princess are duplicated almost perfectly.

Legs

The fake Legs is slightly lighter in color. The hang tag and tush tag are a bit larger.

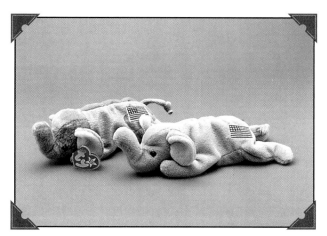

Righty

The counterfeit Righty is poorly done. The fabric is darker with a different feel to the plush.

In these photos the authentic Beanie Baby* is on the right, the fake on the left.

· ·

Peking

The counterfeit Peking's nose comes more to a point and the patches around his eyes droop down rather than stick out sideways. The tags are also often done wrong including some that have a "u" instead of a "ü" in the word Nürnberg. Nürnberg is the site of one of Ty's* headquarters and is listed on the left inside portion of some 2nd and 3rd generation hang tags. This misspelling is common with many counterfeits.

Royal Blue Peanut

This counterfeit royal blue Peanut is poorly done. A light blue Peanut was used and dyed darker.

Coral

This Coral, which was ordered on the Internet directly from China, was a good reproduction. The ink on the tush tag was lighter though and the fins are slightly different.

COUNTERFEITS

The authentic Beanie Baby* is on the right, the fake on the left.

• •

Grunt

Counterfeit Grunts are much smaller and the nose is shaped differently. Their tags are often poorly duplicated. Most counterfeit Grunts are underfilled so to appear scrawnier.

Kiwi

The easiest way to spot a fake Kiwi is by the size of his beak. The fakes have a much shorter beak that barely touches the red on his chest. The authentic Kiwi's beak goes about 1" to 1½" past the beginning of the red on his chest.

Chops

The counterfeit Chops has a much scrawnier body and the material feels different. The size of the fake is not at all similar to the real Chops. Compare one to a real Chops and you will see an obvious difference.

Red Pinky

Who is she? Red Pinkys began showing up on the secondary market in late 1997. No one seems to know where she came from. Most dealers feel she is a counterfeit manufacturing oddity. Others feel she may be a Ty* factory reject.

Other than color, at first glance red Pinky appears to be a close replica of the authentic Ty* Pinky. The body style is the same, but this Pinky's body is red instead of pink. The legs are light pink as is the underside of the wings. The body appears to be under-stuffed. The tush tag's ink is lighter in color.

We question the authenticity of this red Pinky. We hope that Ty* will officially solve this dilemma by responding to our question of its origin.

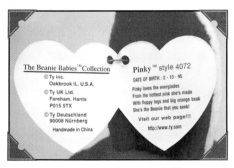

*Trademark or name of Ty, Inc., McDonald's Corporation or other distributors of Ty, Inc. dolls, not affiliated with the authors or Schroeder Publishing.

There is no way to get a picture of every counterfeit, but we have shown examples of many of the most common ones. Some other Beanies* which have been counterfeited are Garcia, OF violet Teddy, Spot without a spot, wingless Quackers, Libearty, Maple, Special Olympic Maple, and Chilly. Even many currents have been counterfeited.

Beanie Baby*
Hang Tags

Hang tags are also known as swing tags or heart tags.
They are attached to the Beanie* with a plastic red or white fastener.

1st Generation
Heart Hang Tag

♥ The only tag that does not open

♥ Produced only in 1994

♥ Thin ty* letters on front

♥ Only tag that is a true heart shape

The Beanie Babies Collection
Brownie ™ Style 4010
© 1993 Ty Inc. Oakbrook, IL. USA
All Rights Reserved. Caution:
Remove this tag before giving
toy to a child. For ages 5 and up.
Handmade in Korea.
Surface
Wash.

2nd Generation
Heart Hang Tag

♥ Introduced in 1994

♥ Same thin ty* letters on front as on 1st generation

♥ Tag opens to double heart

♥ "To____ and from____ , with love" added to some tags

♥ Some tags produced without "To____, From____, with love"

The Beanie Babies Collection
© 1993 Ty Inc. Oakbrook, IL. USA
All Rights Reserved. Caution:
Remove this tag before giving
toy to a child. For ages 3 and up.
Handmade in China
Surface
Wash

Quacker ™ style 4024
to____
from____
with
love

3rd Generation Heart Hang Tag

♥ Introduced in mid-1995

♥ ty* on front much larger

♥ Still included "to_____ and from_____ , with love"

4th Generation Heart Hang Tag

♥ Introduced mid-1996

♥ ty* on front no longer edged in gold

♥ Birthday and poem added

♥ "To_____ and from_____" was deleted

5th Generation Heart Hang Tag

♥ Introduced January 1998

♥ Font changed

♥ Trademark changed to "The Beanie Babies Collection®"*

♥ Style number no longer given (but is included in UPC code)

♥ Beanie* name centered

♥ Birthday month spelled full (such as July 1, 1996)

Beanie Baby* Hang Tag Chart

STYLE #	BEANIE BABY* NAME	1st Generation	2nd Generation	3rd Generation	4th Generation	5th Generation
4032	Ally	●	●	●	●	
4195	Ants					●
4074	Baldy				●	●
4035	Batty				●	●
4109	Bernie				●	●
4009	Bessie			●	●	●
4011	Blackie	●	●	●	●	●
4163	Blizzard				●	●
4001	Bones	●	●	●	●	●
4067	Bongo - tan tail			●	●	
4067	Bongo - brown tail			●	●	
4601	Britannia					●
4085	Bronty			●		
4010	Brownie	●				
4183	Bruno					●
4078	Bubbles			●	●	
4016	Bucky			●	●	●
4045	Bumble			●	●	
4071	Caw			●		
4012	Chilly	●	●	●		
4121	Chip				●	●
4015	Chocolate	●	●	●	●	●
4019	Chops			●	●	
4083	Claude				●	●
4160	Congo				●	●
4079	Coral			●	●	
4130	Crunch				●	●
4010	Cubbie	●	●	●	●	●
4052	Curly				●	●
4006	Daisy	●	●	●	●	●
4008	Derby - fine-mane			●		
4008	Derby - coarse-mane			●	●	
4008	Derby - coarse-main, star					●
4027	Digger - orange	●	●	●		
4027	Digger - red			●	●	
4110	Doby				●	●
4171	Doodle				●	
4100	Dotty				●	●

272

STYLE #	BEANIE BABY* NAME	1st Generation	2nd Generation	3rd Generation	4th Generation	5th Generation
4190	Early					●
4018	Ears			●	●	●
4180	Echo				●	●
4186	Erin					●
4189	Fetch					●
4021	Flash	●	●	●	●	
4125	Fleece				●	●
4012	Flip			●	●	
4118	Floppity - lavender				●	●
4043	Flutter			●		
4196	Fortune					●
4066	Freckles				●	●
4051	Garcia			●	●	
4191	Gigi					●
4188	Glory					●
4034	Gobbles				●	●
4023	Goldie	●	●	●	●	●
4126	Gracie				●	●
4092	Grunt			●	●	
4061	Happy - gray	●	●	●		
4061	Happy - lavender			●	●	●
4119	Hippity - mint				●	●
4185	Hissy					●
4073	Hoot			●	●	
4117	Hoppity - pink				●	●
4060	Humphrey	●	●	●		
4038	Iggy					●
4044	Inch - felt antennas			●	●	
4044	Inch - yarn antennas				●	●
4028	Inky - tan without a mouth	●	●			
4028	Inky - tan with mouth			●		
4028	Inky - pink			●	●	●
4197	Jabber					●
4199	Jake					●
4082	Jolly				●	●
4070	Kiwi			●	●	
4192	Kuku					●
4085	Lefty				●	
4020	Legs	●	●	●	●	
4057	Libearty				●	
4033	Lizzy - tie-dyed			●		

BEANIE BABY* HANG TAG CHART

STYLE #	BEANIE BABY* NAME	1st Generation	2nd Generation	3rd Generation	4th Generation	5th Generation
4033	Lizzy - blue			●	●	●
4040	Lucky - 7 dots	●	●	●		
4040	Lucky - 11 dots				●	●
4040	Lucky - 21 dots				●	
4088	Magic - light pink stitching			●	●	
4088	Magic - hot pink stitching				●	
4081	Manny			●	●	
4600	Maple / Pride				●	
4600	Maple / Maple				●	
4600	Maple / Special Olympics				●	
4162	Mel				●	●
4007	Mystic - fine-mane	●	●	●		
4007	Mystic - coarse-mane			●	●	
4007	Mystic - coarse-mane-iridescent					●
4067	Nana			●		
4104	Nanook				●	●
4003	Nip - gold/white belly		●	●		
4003	Nip - all gold			●		
4003	Nip - gold/white paws			●	●	●
4114	Nuts				●	●
4025	Patti - deep fuchsia	●	●			
4025	Patti - raspberry	●	●			
4025	Patti - magenta			●		
4025	Patti - fuchsia			●	●	●
4053	Peace				●	●
4062	Peanut - royal blue			●		
4062	Peanut - light blue			●	●	●
4013	Peking	●	●	●		
4026	Pinchers	●	●	●	●	●
4072	Pinky		●		●	●
4161	Pouch				●	●
4122	Pounce					●
4123	Prance					●
4300	Princess	SPECIAL MEMORIAL TRIBUTE HANG TAG				
4181	Puffer					●
4106	Pugsly				●	●
4026	Punchers	●				
4024	Quackers - without wings	●				
4024	Quacker - without wings		●			
4024	Quacker - with wings		●			
4024	Quackers - with wings			●	●	●

STYLE #	BEANIE BABY* NAME	1st Generation	2nd Generation	3rd Generation	4th Generation	5th Generation
4091	Radar			●	●	
4037	Rainbow					●
4086	Rex			●		
4086	Righty				●	
4014	Ringo			●	●	●
4069	Roary				●	
4202	Rocket					●
4101	Rover				●	●
4107	Scoop				●	●
4102	Scottie				●	●
4029	Seamore	●	●	●	●	
4080	Seaweed			●	●	●
4031	Slither	●	●	●		
4115	Sly - brown bellied				●	
4115	Sly - white bellied				●	●
4034	Smoochy					●
4120	Snip				●	●
4002	Snort				●	●
4201	Snowball				●	
4100	Sparky				●	
4030	Speedy	●	●	●	●	
4060	Spike				●	●
4022	Splash	●	●	●	●	
4036	Spinner					●
4090	Spook			●		
4090	Spooky			●	●	
4000	Spot - without spot	●	●			
4000	Spot - with spot		●	●	●	
4184	Spunky					●
4005	Squealer	●	●	●	●	●
4087	Steg			●		
4077	Sting			●	●	
4193	Stinger					●
4017	Stinky			●		●
4082	Stretch					●
4065	Stripes - gold & black			●		
4065	Stripes - gold & black-fuzzy belly			●		
4065	Stripes - caramel and black				●	●
4171	Strut					●
4002	Tabasco			●	●	
4031	Tank - 7 - line no shell			●	●	
4031	Tank - 9 - line no shell				●	

BEANIE BABY* HANG TAG CHART

STYLE #	BEANIE BABY* NAME	1st Generation	2nd Generation	3rd Generation	4th Generation	5th Generation
4031	Tank - 7 - line with shell				●	
4200	Teddy 97				●	
4055	Teddy - OF brown	●	●			
4052	Teddy - OF cranberry	●	●			
4057	Teddy - OF jade	●	●			
4056	Teddy - OF magenta	●	●			
4051	Teddy - OF teal	●	●			
4055	Teddy - OF violet	●	●			
4050	Teddy - NF brown		●	●	●	
4052	Teddy - NF cranberry		●	●		
4057	Teddy - NF jade		●	●		
4056	Teddy - NF magenta		●	●		
4051	Teddy - NF teal		●	●		
4055	Teddy - NF violet		●	●		
4198	Tracker	●	●			●
4042	Trap			●		
4076	Tuck				●	
4108	Tuffy				●	●
4076	Tusk			●	●	
4068	Twigs			●	●	●
4058	Valentino		●	●	●	●
4064	Velvet			●	●	
4075	Waddle			●	●	●
4084	Waves				●	●
4041	Web	●	●	●		
4013	Weenie			●	●	●
4194	Whisper					●
4187	Wise					●
4103	Wrinkles				●	●
4063	Ziggy			●	●	●
4004	Zip - black/white belly		●	●		
4004	Zip - all black			●		
4004	Zip - black/white paws			●	●	●

276

BEANIE BABY*
TUSH TAGS

Tush tags are the sewn tags on the Beanie Baby*.

© 1995 TY INC.,
OAKBROOK IL. U.S.A.
ALL RIGHTS RESERVED
HAND MADE IN CHINA
SURFACE WASHABLE

ALL NEW MATERIAL
POLYESTER FIBER
& P.V.C. PELLETS CE
PA. REG # 1965

FIRST GENERATION

ty ®

HAND MADE IN CHINA
© 1993 TY INC.,
OAKBROOK IL. U. S. A.
SURFACE WASHABLE
ALL NEW MATERIAL
POLYESTER FIBER &
P. V.C. PELLETS
REG. NO. PA-1965(KR)
FOR AGES 3 AND UP
CE

SECOND GENERATION

The
Beanie Babies
Collection™

ty ®

Scottie

HANDMADE IN CHINA
© 1996 TY INC.,
OAKBROOK IL, U.S.A
SURFACE WASHABLE
ALL NEW MATERIAL
POLYESTER FIBER
& P.V.C PELLETS CE
REG. NO PA. 1965(KR)

THIRD GENERATION

The
Beanie Babies
Collection™

★**ty** ®

Inky

HANDMADE IN CHINA
© 1993 TY INC.,
OAKBROOK IL, U.S.A
SURFACE WASHABLE
ALL NEW MATERIAL
POLYESTER FIBER
& P.V.C PELLETS CE
REG. NO PA. 1965(KR)

FOURTH GENERATION

The
Beanie Babies ®
Collection™

★**ty** ®

Gobbles™

HANDMADE IN CHINA
© 1996 TY INC.,
OAKBROOK IL, U.S.A.
SURFACE WASHABLE
ALL NEW MATERIAL
POLYESTER FIBER
& P.V.C. PELLETS CE
REG. NO PA. 1965(KR)

FIFTH GENERATION

The
Beanie Babies
Collection ®

★**ty** ®

Ants™

HANDMADE IN CHINA
© 1998 TY INC.,
OAKBROOK, IL. U.S.A.
SURFACE WASHABLE
ALL NEW MATERIAL
POLYESTER FIBER
& P.E. PELLETS CE
REG. NO PA. 1965(KR)

安庭玩具厂
(223)
*

SEVENTH GENERATION

The
Beanie Babies
Collection ®

★**ty** ®

Spunky™

HANDMADE IN CHINA
© 1997 TY INC.,
OAKBROOK, IL. U.S.A.
SURFACE WASHABLE
ALL NEW MATERIAL
POLYESTER FIBER
& P.E. PELLETS CE
REG. NO PA. 1965(KR)

SIXTH GENERATION

Not to be removed until delivered to the consumer	Ne pas enlever avant livraison au consommateur
This label is affixed in compliance with the Upholstered and Stuffed Articles Act	Cette étiquette est apposée conformément à loi sur les articles rembourrés
This article contains NEW MATERIAL ONLY	Cet article contient MATÉRIAU NEUF SEULEMENT
Made by Ont. Reg. No.	Fabriqué par No d'enrg. Ont.
20B6484	20B6484
Content: Plastic Pellets Polyester Fibers	Contenut: Boulette de plastique Fibres de Polyester
Made in China	Fabriqué en Chine

CANADIAN TUSH TAG

FIRST GENERATION
- Produced 1993 – 1995
- Black lettering
- No Beanie* name

SECOND GENERATION
- Produced 1995 – 1996
- Red lettering
- Ty* heart logo
- Wider tag than others
- No 1994 tag was made
- Tag may say 1993 despite being produced in 1995 – 96
- No Beanie* name

THIRD GENERATION
- Produced 1996 – 1997
- Smaller heart
- Name of Beanie* added
- "The Beanie Babies Collection™" added
- Tag may say 1993 or 1995, 1996

FOURTH GENERATION
- Produced mid 1997 – 1998
- Small star added left of ty heart
- Star often added by clear sticker on 3rd Generation tush tags

FIFTH GENERATION
- Trademark symbol, ™, added to Beanie* name
- Uses "®" after "Beanie Babies"*

SIXTH GENERATION
- Now reads "Beanie Babies Collection®"
- Produced in 1998 but may say "1995 – 1998"

SEVENTH GENERATION
- Same as sixth generation except has added stamp on inside

CANADIAN
- Canadian Beanies* have an additional larger black and white tag along with their regular tush tags. The information is in both French and English. All Beanie Babies* made to be sold in Canada have this additional tag.

BEANIE BABY* TUSH TAG CHART

STYLE #	BEANIE BABY* NAME	1st Generation		2nd Generation		3rd Generation		4th Generation	5th Generation	6th Generation	7th Generation
		1993 b/w	1995 b/w	1993 red No Name	1995 red No Name	1993 red W/ Name	1995 red W/ Name	Red With Name And Star	Red With Name	Red With Name	Inside Stamp
4032	Ally	●		●		●					
4195	Ants									●	●
4074	Baldy							●	●	●	
4035	Batty								●	●	●
4109	Bernie							●	●	●	
4009	Bessie		●		●		●	●			
4011	Blackie	●		●		●		●	●	●	●
4163	Blizzard							●	●		
4001	Bones	●		●		●		●	●		
4067	Bongo - tan tail		●		●		●		●	●	
4067	Bongo - brown tail				●		●				
4601	Britannia									●	●
4085	Bronty		●		●						
4010	Brownie	●									
4183	Bruno								●	●	●
4078	Bubbles		●		●		●				
4016	Bucky				●		●	●	●		
4045	Bumble		●		●		●				
4071	Caw		●		●						
4012	Chilly		●								
4121	Chip							●	●	●	●
4015	Chocolate	●		●		●		●	●	●	●
4019	Chops				●		●				
4083	Claude							●			●
4160	Congo							●	●	●	●
4079	Coral		●		●		●				
4130	Crunch							●	●	●	●
4010	Cubbie	●		●		●		●	●		
4052	Curly						●	●	●	●	●
4006	Daisy	●		●		●		●	●	●	●
4008	Derby - fine-mane		●			●					
4008	Derby - coarse-mane		●			●		●	●		

278

BEANIE BABY* TUSH TAG CHART

STYLE #	BEANIE BABY* NAME	1st Generation		2nd Generation		3rd Generation		4th Generation	5th Generation	6th Generation	7th Generation
		1993 b/w	1995 b/w	1993 red No Name	1995 red No Name	1993 red W/Name	1995 red W/Name	Red With Name And Star	Red With Name	Red With Name	Inside Stamp
4008	Derby - coarse-mane, star								●	●	●
4027	Digger - orange	●									
4027	Digger - red	●		●		●		●			
4110	Doby							●	●	●	●
4171	Doodle							●			
4100	Dotty							●	●	●	●
4190	Early									●	●
4018	Ears				●		●				
4180	Echo							●	●	●	
4186	Erin									●	●
4189	Fetch										●
4021	Flash	●		●		●		●			
4125	Fleece							●	●		●
4012	Flip			●		●		●	●		
4118	Floppity - lavender							●	●	●	
4043	Flutter		●		●						
4196	Fortune									●	●
4066	Freckles							●	●	●	●
4051	Garcia			●		●					
4191	Gigi									●	●
4188	Glory									●	●
4034	Gobbles								●		
4023	Goldie	●		●		●		●	●		
4126	Gracie							●	●	●	
4092	Grunt				●		●	●			
4061	Happy - gray	●									
4061	Happy - lavender	●		●		●		●	●	●	
4119	Hippity - mint							●	●	●	
4185	Hissy									●	●
4073	Hoot				●		●	●	●		
4117	Hoppity - pink							●	●	●	
4060	Humphrey	●									
4038	Iggy									●	●
4038	Iggy - with tongue										●
4044	Inch - felt antennas		●		●		●				

Beanie Baby* Tush Tag Chart

STYLE #	BEANIE BABY* NAME	1st Generation		2nd Generation		3rd Generation		4th Generation	5th Generation	6th Generation	7th Generation
		1993 b/w	1995 b/w	1993 red No Name	1995 red No Name	1993 red W/ Name	1995 red W/ Name	Red With Name And Star	Red With Name	Red With Name	Inside Stamp
4044	Inch - yarn antennas						●	●	●	●	
4028	Inky - tan w/o a mouth	●									
4028	Inky - tan with mouth	●									
4028	Inky - pink	●		●		●		●	●	●	
4197	Jabber									●	●
4199	Jake									●	●
4082	Jolly							●	●	●	
4070	Kiwi		●		●		●				
4192	Kuku									●	●
4085	Lefty							●			
4020	Legs	●	●	●				●	●		
4057	Libearty							●			
4033	Lizzy - tie-dyed		●								
4033	Lizzy - blue							●	●	●	
4040	Lucky - 7 spots	●	●								
4040	Lucky - 11 spots						●	●	●	●	
4040	Lucky - 21 spots						●				
4088	Magic - light pink stitch.		●		●		●	●	●		
4088	Magic - hot pink stitch.						●				
4081	Manny				●		●				
4600	Maple/Pride							●			
4600	Maple/Maple							●	●	●	●
4600	Maple/Special Olympics							●			
4162	Mel							●	●	●	●
4007	Mystic - fine-mane	●		●							
4007	Mystic - coarse-mane	●		●		●		●	●		
4007	Mystic - coarse-mane-irid.									●	●
4067	Nana		●								
4104	Nanook							●	●	●	
4003	Nip - gold/white belly	●									
4003	Nip - all gold	●									
4003	Nip - gold/white paws			●		●		●	●		
4114	Nuts							●	●	●	●
4025	Patti - deep fuchsia	●									
4025	Patti - raspberry	●									

BEANIE BABY* TUSH TAG CHART

STYLE #	BEANIE BABY* NAME	1st Generation		2nd Generation		3rd Generation		4th Generation	5th Generation	6th Generation	7th Generation
		1993 b/w	1995 b/w	1993 red No Name	1995 red No Name	1993 red W/ Name	1995 red W/ Name	Red With Name And Star	Red With Name	Red With Name	Inside Stamp
4025	Patti - magenta	●									
4025	Patti - fuchsia	●		●		●		●	●	●	
4053	Peace							●	●		●
4062	Peanut - royal blue		●								
4062	Peanut - light blue		●		●		●	●	●	●	
4013	Peking	●									
4026	Pinchers	●		●		●		●	●	●	
4072	Pinky		●		●		●	●	●	●	●
4161	Pouch							●	●	●	
4122	Pounce									●	●
4123	Prance									●	●
4300	Princess								●	●	●
4181	Puffer									●	●
4106	Pugsly							●	●		●
4026	Punchers	●									
4024	Quackers - w/o wings	●									
4024	Quacker - w/o wings	●									
4024	Quacker - with wings	●									
4024	Quackers - with wings	●		●		●		●	●	●	
4091	Radar		●		●		●				
4037	Rainbow									●	●
4086	Rex		●		●						
4086	Righty							●			
4014	Ringo				●		●	●	●	●	●
4069	Roary							●	●	●	
4202	Rocket									●	●
4101	Rover							●	●	●	
4107	Scoop							●	●	●	●
4102	Scottie							●	●	●	
4029	Seamore	●		●		●					
4080	Seaweed							●	●	●	●
4031	Slither	●									
4115	Sly - brown bellied										
4115	Sly - white bellied							●	●	●	●
4034	Smoochy									●	●

281

BEANIE BABY* TUSH TAG CHART

STYLE #	BEANIE BABY* NAME	1st Generation		2nd Generation		3rd Generation		4th Generation	5th Generation	6th Generation	7th Generation
		1993 b/w	1995 b/w	1993 red No Name	1995 red No Name	1993 red W/ Name	1995 red W/ Name	Red With Name And Star	Red With Name	Red With Name	Inside Stamp
4120	Snip							●	●	●	●
4002	Snort							●	●	●	●
4201	Snowball								●		
4100	Sparky							●			
4030	Speedy	●		●		●		●	●		
4060	Spike							●	●	●	●
4022	Splash	●		●		●		●			
4036	Spinner								●	●	●
4090	Spook		●		●						
4090	Spooky		●		●		●	●	●		
4000	Spot - without spot	●									
4000	Spot - with spot	●		●		●		●	●		
4184	Spunky									●	●
4005	Squealer	●		●		●		●	●	●	
4087	Steg		●		●						
4077	Sting		●		●		●	●			
4193	Stinger									●	●
4017	Stinky		●		●		●	●	●	●	●
4082	Stretch									●	●
4065	Stripes - gold & blk		●		●						
4065	Stripes - gold & blk-fuzzy belly		●		●						
4065	Stripes - caramel & blk				●		●	●	●	●	
4171	Strut								●	●	●
4002	Tabasco		●		●		●				
4031	Tank - 7-line no shell		●		●		●				
4031	Tank - 9-line no shell						●				
4031	Tank - 7-line with shell							●	●		
4200	Teddy 97								●		
4055	Teddy - OF brown	●									
4052	Teddy - OF cranberry	●									
4057	Teddy - OF jade	●									
4056	Teddy - OF magenta	●									
4051	Teddy - OF teal	●									
4055	Teddy - OF violet	●									
4050	Teddy - NF brown	●		●		●		●	●		

BEANIE BABY* TUSH TAG CHART

STYLE #	BEANIE BABY* NAME	1st Generation		2nd Generation		3rd Generation		4th Generation	5th Generation	6th Generation	7th Generation
		1993 b/w	1995 b/w	1993 red No Name	1995 red No Name	1993 red W/ Name	1995 red W/ Name	Red With Name And Star	Red With Name	Red With Name	Inside Stamp
4052	Teddy - NF cranberry	●									
4057	Teddy - NF jade	●									
4056	Teddy - NF magenta	●									
4051	Teddy - NF teal	●									
4055	Teddy - NF violet	●									
4198	Tracker									●	●
4042	Trap	●									
4076	Tuck						●				
4108	Tuffy							●			
4076	Tusk		●		●		●	●			
4068	Twigs			●		●			●	●	
4058	Valentino	●		●		●		●	●	●	●
4064	Velvet		●		●			●	●		
4075	Waddle		●		●		●	●	●	●	
4084	Waves							●	●	●	
4041	Web	●									
4013	Weenie				●		●	●	●	●	
4194	Whisper									●	●
4187	Wise									●	●
4103	Wrinkles							●	●	●	●
4063	Ziggy		●		●		●	●	●	●	
4004	Zip - black/white belly	●									
4004	Zip - all black	●									
4004	Zip - black/white paws			●		●		●	●	●	

1997
BEANIE BABIES*
RETIREES

JANUARY '97

MAY '97

OCTOBER '97

1998
Beanie Babies[*]
Retirees

· ·

JANUARY '98

MAY '98

BEANIE BABIES*
RETIRED AND OUT OF PRODUCTION

1993
Brownie
Patti - deep fuchsia
Punchers

1994
Inky - tan without a mouth
Patti - raspberry
Spot - without a spot

1995
Chilly
Derby - fine-mane
Digger - orange
Happy - gray
Humphrey
Inky - tan with a mouth
Lizzy - tie-dyed
Mystic - fine-mane
Nana
Nip - all gold
Nip - white belly
Patti - magenta
Peanut - royal blue
Peking
Quackers without wings
Slither
Spook
Teddy, old face cranberry
Teddy, old face jade
Teddy, old face brown
Teddy, old face magenta
Teddy, old face teal
Teddy, old face violet
Teddy, new face cranberry
Teddy, new face jade
Teddy, new face magenta
Teddy, new face teal
Teddy, new face violet
Trap
Web
Zip - all black
Zip - white belly

1996
Bongo - brown tail, red tush, no name
Bongo - tan tail, B&W tush
Bongo - tan tail, red tush, no name
Bronty
Bumble
Caw
Flutter
Inch - felt
Lucky - 7 spot
Rex
Sly - brown belly
Steg
Stripes - gold and black
Tank - 7 line
Tank - 9 line

1997
Ally
Bessie
Bubbles
Chops
Coral
Digger - red
Doodle
Flash
Flip
Garcia
Grunt
Hoot
Kiwi
Lefty
Legs
Libearty
Manny
Mystic - coarse-mane, tan horn
Radar
Righty
Seamore
Sparky
Speedy
Splash
Spot
Sting
Tabasco
Tank
Teddy, new face brown
Tusk
Velvet

1998
Baldy
Blizzard
Bones
Bucky
Cubbie
Derby - coarse-mane
Ears
Echo
Floppity
Goldie
Gracie
Happy - lavender
Hippity
Hoppity
Inch - yarn
Inky - pink
Jolly
Lizzie - blue
Lucky - 11 spot
Magic
Nip - white paws
Patti - fuchsia
Peanut - light blue
Pinchers
Quackers
Rover
Scottie
Snowball
Spooky
Squealer
Stripes - caramel and black
97 Teddy
Twigs
Waddle
Waves
Weenie
Ziggy
Zip - white paws

BEANIE BABIES*
BIRTHDAYS

Jan
Jan. 3, 1993: Spot
Jan. 5, 1997: Kuku
Jan. 6, 1993: Patti
Jan. 13, 1996: Crunch
Jan. 14, 1997: Spunky
Jan. 15, 1996: Mel
Jan. 18, 1994: Bones
Jan. 21, 1996: Nuts
Jan. 25, 1995: Peanut
Jan. 26, 1996: Chip

Feb
Feb. 1, 1996: Peace
Feb. 4, 1997: Fortune
Feb. 13, 1995: Pinky
Feb. 13, 1995: Stinky
Feb. 14, 1994: Valentino
Feb. 17, 1996: Baldy
Feb. 20, 1996: Roary
Feb. 22, 1995: Tank
Feb. 25, 1994: Happy
Feb. 27, 1996: Sparky
Feb. 28, 1995: Flip

Mar
Mar. 2, 1995: Coral
Mar. 4, 1997: Fetch
Mar. 6, 1994: Nip
Mar. 8, 1996: Doodle
Mar. 8, 1996: Strut
Mar. 12, 1997: Rocket
Mar. 14, 1994: Ally
Mar. 19, 1996: Seaweed
Mar. 20, 1997: Early
Mar. 21, 1996: Fleece
Mar. 28, 1994: Zip

Apr
Apr. 3, 1996: Hoppity
Apr. 4, 1997: Hissy
Apr. 5, 1997: Whisper
Apr. 7, 1997: Gigi
Apr. 12, 1996: Curly
Apr. 16, 1997: Jake
Apr. 18, 1995: Ears
Apr. 19, 1994: Quackers
Apr. 23, 1993: Squealer
Apr. 25, 1993: Legs
Apr. 27, 1993: Chocolate

May
May 1, 1995: Lucky
May 1, 1996: Wrinkles
May 2, 1996: Pugsly
May 3, 1996: Chops
May 10, 1994: Daisy
May 11, 1995: Lizzy
May 13, 1993: Flash
May 15, 1995: Tabasco
May 15, 1995: Snort
May 19, 1995: Twigs
May 21, 1994: Mystic
May 28, 1996: Floppity
May 30, 1996: Rover
May 31, 1997: Wise

Jun
June 1, 1996: Hippity
June 3, 1996: Freckles
June 5, 1997: Tracker
June 8, 1995: Bucky
June 8, 1995: Manny
June 11, 1995: Stripes
June 15, 1996: Scottie
June 17, 1996: Gracie
June 19, 1993: Pinchers
June 27, 1995: Bessie

BEANIE BABIES*
BIRTHDAYS

Jul

July 1, 1996: Maple
July 1, 1996: Pride
July 1, 1996: Scoop
July 2, 1995: Bubbles
July 4, 1997: Glory
July 4, 1996: Lefty
July 4, 1996: Righty
July 8, 1993: Splash
July 14, 1995: Ringo
July 15, 1994: Blackie
July 19, 1995: Grunt
July 20, 1995: Weenie

Aug

Aug. 1, 1995: Garcia
Aug. 9, 1995: Hoot
Aug. 12, 1997: Iggy
Aug. 13, 1996: Spike
Aug. 14, 1994: Speedy
Aug. 17, 1995: Bongo
Aug. 23, 1995: Digger
Aug. 27, 1995: Sting
Aug. 28, 1997: Pounce

Summer 1996: Libearty

Sept

Sept. 3, 1995: Inch
Sept. 3, 1996: Claude
Sept. 5, 1995: Magic
Sept. 9, 1997: Bruno
Sept. 12, 1996: Sly
Sept. 16, 1995: Kiwi
Sept. 16, 1995: Derby
Sept. 18, 1995: Tusk
Sept. 21, 1997: Stretch
Sept. 29, 1997: Stinger

Oct

Oct. 1, 1997: Smoochy
Oct. 3, 1996: Bernie
Oct. 9, 1996: Doby
Oct. 10, 1997: Jabber
Oct. 12, 1996: Tuffy
Oct. 14, 1997: Rainbow
Oct. 16, 1995: Bumble
Oct. 17. 1996: Dotty
Oct. 22, 1996: Snip
Oct. 28, 1996: Spinner
Oct. 29, 1996: Batty
Oct. 30, 1995: Radar
Oct. 31, 1995: Spooky

Nov

Nov. 3, 1997: Puffer
Nov. 6, 1996: Pouch
Nov. 7, 1997: Ants
Nov. 9, 1996: Congo
Nov. 14, 1993: Cubbie
Nov. 14, 1994: Goldie
Nov. 20, 1997: Prance
Nov. 21, 1996: Nanook
Nov. 27, 1996: Gobbles
Nov. 28, 1995: Teddy Brown
Nov. 29, 1994: Inky

Dec

Dec. 2, 1996: Jolly
Dec. 8, 1996: Waves
Dec. 12, 1996: Blizzard
Dec. 14, 1996: Seamore
Dec. 16, 1995: Velvet
Dec. 19, 1995: Waddle
Dec. 21, 1996: Echo
Dec. 22, 1996: Snowball
Dec. 24, 1995: Ziggy
Dec. 25, 1996: 1997 Teddy

BEANIE BABIES*
INTERNET SITES
. . . .

Ty Inc.*
http://www.ty.com

Beanie Mom
http://www.beaniemom.com

The Beanie Encyclopedia
http://www.beanieencyclopedia.net

Toys For Toddlers
http://www.toysfortoddlers.com

Kim and Kevin's Collectibles
http://www.knkcollectibles.com

Paul and Judy's Coins and Cards
http://www.pjcc.com

E-Bay Auction
http://www.ebay.com

Auction Universe
http://www.auctionuniverse.com

Up 4 Sale
http://www.up4sale.com

Lemon Lainey Design In England
http://www.lemonlaineydesign.com

BEANIE BABIES* CHECKLIST

	Ally, the alligator ●		Digger, the orange crab ●
	Ants, the anteater		Digger, the red crab ●
	Baldy, the eagle ●		Doby, the doberman
	Batty, the bat		Doodle, the rooster ●
	Bernie, the St. Bernard		Dotty, the Dalmatian
	Bessie, the brown and white cow ●		Early, the robin
	Blackie, the black bear		Ears, the brown rabbit ●
	Blizzard, the black and white tiger ●		Echo, the dolphin ●
	Bones, the brown dog ●		Erin, the bear
	Bongo, the monkey/brown tail ●		Fetch, the golden retriever
	Bongo, the monkey/tan tail		Flash, the dolphin ●
	Britannia, the bear		Fleece, the lamb
	Bronty, the brontosaurus ●		Flip, the white cat ●
	Brownie, the brown bear ●		Floppity, the lavender bunny ●
	Bruno, the terrier		Flutter, the butterfly ●
	Bubbles, the black and yellow fish ●		Fortune, the panda bear
	Bucky, the beaver ●		Freckles, the leopard
	Bumble, the bee ●		Garcia, the bear ●
	Caw, the crow ●		Gigi, the poodle
	Chilly, the polar bear ●		Glory, the bear
	Chip, the calico cat		Gobbles, the turkey
	Chocolate, the moose		Goldie, the goldfish ●
	Chops, the lamb ●		Gracie, the swan ●
	Claude, the tie-dyed crab		Grunt, the razorback ●
	Congo, the gorilla		Happy, the gray hippo ●
	Coral, the tie-dyed fish ●		Happy, the lavender hippo ●
	Crunch, the shark		Hippity, the mint green bunny ●
	Cubbie, the brown bear ●		Hissy, the snake
	Curly, the brown napped bear		Hoot, the owl ●
	Daisy, the black and white cow		Hoppity, the pink bunny ●
	Derby, the coarse-mane horse ●		Humphrey, the camel ●
	Derby, the fine-mane horse ●		Iggy, the iguana
	Derby, the coarse-mane horse, star		Iggy, the iguana with tongue

BEANIE BABIES* CHECKLIST

Inch, the inchworm with felt antennas ●	Patti, the fuchsia platypus ●
Inch, the inchworm with yarn antennas ●	Patti, the magenta platypus ●
Inky, the pink octopus ●	Patti, the raspberry platypus ●
Inky, the tan octopus with a mouth ●	Peace, the bear
Inky, the tan octopus without a mouth ●	Peanut, the light blue elephant ●
Jabber, the parrot	Peanut, the royal blue elephant ●
Jake, the mallard duck	Peking, the panda bear ●
Jolly, the walrus ●	Pinchers, the lobster ●
Kiwi, the toucan ●	Pinky, the flamingo
Kuku, the cockatoo	Pouch, the kangaroo
Lefty, the donkey ●	Pounce, the brown cat
Legs, the frog ●	Prance, the gray cat
Libearty, the bear ●	Princess, the bear
Lizzy, the blue lizard ●	Puffer, the puffin
Lizzy, the tie-dyed lizard ●	Pugsly, the pug dog
Lucky, the ladybug with 7 felt spots ●	Punchers, the lobster ●
Lucky, the ladybug with 11 spots ●	Quackers, the duck with wings ●
Lucky, the ladybug with 21 spots ●	Quackers, the duck without wings ●
Magic, the dragon hot pink stitching ●	Radar, the bat ●
Magic, the dragon light pink stitching ●	Rainbow, the chameleon
Manny, the manatee ●	Rex, the tyrannosaurus ●
Maple/Maple, the Canadian bear	Righty, the elephant ●
Maple/Pride the Canadian flag bear ●	Ringo, the raccoon
Maple - Special Olympics ●	Roary, the lion
Mel, the koala	Rocket, the blue jay
Mystic, the coarse-mane unicorn ●	Rover, the dog ●
Mystic, the fine-mane unicorn ●	Scoop, the pelican
Mystic, the coarse-mane unicorn - iridescent	Scottie, the Sottish terrier ●
Nana, the monkey ●	Seamore, the seal ●
Nanook, the husky	Seaweed, the otter
Nip, the gold cat ●	Slither, the snake ●
Nip, the gold cat with white face and belly ●	Sly, the brown bellied fox ●
Nip, the gold cat with white paws ●	Sly, the white bellied fox
Nuts, the squirrel	Smoochy, the frog
Patti, the deep fuchsia platypus ●	Snip, the Siamese cat

BEANIE BABIES* CHECKLIST

	Snort, the bull		Teddy, the new face-magenta bear ●
	Snowball, the snowman ●		Teddy, the new face-teal bear ●
	Sparky, the Dalmatian ●		Teddy, the new face-violet bear ●
	Speedy, the turtle ●		Teddy, the old face-brown bear ●
	Spike, the rhinoceros		Teddy, the old face-cranberry bear ●
	Spinner, the spider		Teddy, the old face-jade bear ●
	Splash, the whale ●		Teddy, the old face-magenta bear ●
	Spook, the ghost ●		Teddy, the old face-teal bear ●
	Spooky, the ghost ●		Teddy, the old face-violet bear ●
	Spot, the dog with a spot ●		Teddy, violet employee bear, green ribbon ●
	Spot, the dog without a spot ●		Teddy, violet employee bear, red ribbon ●
	Spunky, the cocker spaniel		Tracker, the basset hound
	Squealer, the pig ●		Trap, the mouse ●
	Steg, the stegosaurus ●		Tuck, the walrus ●
	Sting, the stingray ●		Tuffy, the terrier
	Stinger, the scorpion		Tusk, the walrus ●
	Stinky, the skunk		Twigs, the giraffe ●
	Stretch, the ostrich		Valentino, the bear
	Stripes, the gold and black tiger ●		Velvet, the panther ●
	Stripes, the gold and black tiger - fuzzy belly ●		Waddle, the penguin ●
	Stripes, the caramel and black tiger ●		Waves, the whale ●
	Strut, the rooster		Web, the spider ●
	Tabasco, the bull ●		Weenie, the dachshund ●
	Tank, the 7-line armadillo ●		Whisper, the deer
	Tank, the 9-line armadillo ●		Wise, the owl
	Tank, the armadillo with shell ●		Wrinkles, the dog
	Teddy -97, Teddy ●		Ziggy, the zebra ●
	Teddy, the new face-brown bear ●		Zip, the all black cat ●
	Teddy, the new face-cranberry bear ●		Zip, the black cat with white face and belly ●
	Teddy, the new face-jade bear ●		Zip, the black cat with white paws ●
			*Trademark or name of Ty, Inc., McDonald's Corporation or other distributors of Ty, Inc. dolls, not affiliated with the authors or Schroeder Publishing.

ACKNOWLEDGMENTS

. . . .

**Thank you to the following people for
their dedication and contributions...**

Michael Carey
Tampa, Florida

Nancy and Jeff Cale,
Franklin, Michigan

Barbara and David Sebring,
White Lake, Michigan

David and Jody Sebring,
Waterford, Michigan

Jim and Corene Sebring,
Ortonville, Michigan

Kelly Byers,
Adventure Comics and Collectibles, Largo, Florida

Mike Lutzow,
Rockton, Illinois

Chester Patterson,
Ocala Flower Shop, Ocala Florida

Christine Tozzo,
Sarasota, Florida

Jaclyn Sporn,
Tampa, Florida

Bear Country Collectibles,
Tampa, Florida

Beth Stanton,
Nicholasville, Kentucky

Cindy Boggs,
Richardson, Texas

Jamie Miller,
Bartlett, Illinois

Jessica Rapp, Lyn Butler, Livent, Inc.
Toronto, Ontario

And A Special Thanks To...
David Hughes - Designer,
HUGHES Advertising, Tampa, Florida

Michael Murphy - Photographer
Tampa, Florida

Richard Logan - Photographer
Tampa, Florida

Lisa Stroup - Editor
Beth Summers
Michelle Dowling
Donna Ballard
Laurie Swick
Collector Books, Paducah, Kentucky

BEANIE BABY* INDEX